T0207411

Lecture Notes in Computer Science 13909

Founding Editors

Gerhard Goos
Juris Hartmanis

Editorial Board Members

The series Lecture Notes in Computer Science (LNCS), including its subseries Lecture Notes in Artificial Intelligence (LNAI) and Lecture Notes in Bioinformatics (LNBI), has established itself as a medium for the publication of new developments in computer science and information technology research, teaching, and education.

LNCS enjoys close cooperation with the computer science R & D community, the series counts many renowned academics among its volume editors and paper authors, and collaborates with prestigious societies. Its mission is to serve this international community by providing an invaluable service, mainly focused on the publication of conference and workshop proceedings and postproceedings. LNCS commenced publication in 1973.

Marta Patiño-Martínez · João Paulo

Editors

Distributed Applications and Interoperable Systems

23rd IFIP WG 6.1 International Conference, DAIS 2023
Held as Part of the 18th International Federated Conference
on Distributed Computing Techniques, DisCoTec 2023
Lisbon, Portugal, June 19–23, 2023
Proceedings

 Springer

Editors
Marta Patiño-Martínez [iD]
Universidad Politécnica de Madrid
Boadilla del Monte, Spain

João Paulo [iD]
University of Minho
Braga, Portugal

ISSN 0302-9743   ISSN 1611-3349 (electronic)
Lecture Notes in Computer Science
ISBN 978-3-031-35259-1   ISBN 978-3-031-35260-7 (eBook)
https://doi.org/10.1007/978-3-031-35260-7

Foreword

The 18th International Federated Conference on Distributed Computing Techniques (DisCoTec) took place in Lisbon, Portugal, from June 19 to June 23, 2023. It was organized by the Department of Computer Science of NOVA School of Science and Technology, NOVA University Lisbon. The DisCoTec series is one of the major events sponsored by the International Federation for Information Processing (IFIP). It comprises three conferences:

- COORDINATION, the IFIP WG 6.1 25th International Conference on Coordination Models and Languages
- DAIS, the IFIP WG 6.1 23rd International Conference on Distributed Applications and Interoperable Systems
- FORTE, the IFIP WG 6.1 43rd International Conference on Formal Techniques for Distributed Objects, Components and Systems

Together, these conferences cover a broad spectrum of distributed computing subjects, ranging from theoretical foundations and formal description techniques to systems research issues. In addition to the individual sessions of each conference, the event also included plenary sessions that gathered attendees from the three conferences. These included joint invited speaker sessions and a joint session for the best papers and artefacts from the three conferences. The keynote speakers of DisCoTec 2023 are listed below:

- Azalea Raad, Imperial College London, UK
- Frank Pfenning, Carnegie Mellon University, USA
- Peter Pietzuch, Imperial College London, UK
- Associated with the federated event were also the following satellite events:
- ICE, the 16th Interaction and Concurrency Experience
- BehAPI Tutorial Day, a series of three tutorials covering results from the BehAPI project

in addition to other short tutorials on relevant topics to DisCoTec.

I would like to thank the Program Committee chairs of the different events for their help and cooperation during the preparation of the conference, and the Steering Committee and Advisory Boards of DisCoTec for their guidance, patience, and support. The organization of DisCoTec 2023 was only possible thanks to the work of the Organizing Committee, including João Costa Seco, João Leitão, Mário Pereira, Carlos Baquero (publicity chair), Simão Melo de Sousa (workshops and tutorials chair), Joana Dâmaso (logistics and finances), as well as all the students who volunteered their time to help. Finally, I would like to thank IFIP WG 6.1 and NOVA LINCS for sponsoring this event,

Springer's Lecture Notes in Computer Science team for their support and sponsorship, and EasyChair for providing the reviewing infrastructure.

June 2023   Carla Ferreira

Preface

This volume contains the papers presented at the 23rd IFIP International Conference on Distributed Applications and Interoperable Systems (DAIS 2023), sponsored by the International Federation for Information Processing (IFIP) and organized by IFIP WG 6.1. The DAIS conference series addresses all practical and conceptual aspects of distributed applications, including their design, modeling, implementation, and operation; the supporting middleware; appropriate software engineering methodologies and tools; and experimental studies and applications. DAIS 2023 was held during June 19–23, 2023, in Lisbon, Portugal, as part of DisCoTec 2023, the 18th International Federated Conference on Distributed Computing Techniques.

We offered three distinct paper tracks: full research papers, full practical experience reports, and work-in-progress papers. We received 13 submissions, all of them for full research papers. All submissions were reviewed by four Program Committee (PC) members. The review process included a post-review discussion phase, during which the merits of all papers were discussed by the PC. The committee decided to accept seven full research papers. Some of these papers went through a shepherding process, led by one of the reviewers of the paper. The accepted papers cover a broad range of topics in distributed computing: algorithms, scalability and availability, deep learning, web3, and edge computing.

This year, we also decided to invite authors of accepted papers to submit publicly available artifacts associated with their papers. This process was chaired by António Sousa and Vinícius Cogo. We received 6 submissions that were reviewed by three Artefact Evaluation Committee (AEC) members. Four submissions were awarded the badges for Reproducibility, Functionality and Availability, two were awarded the Availability and Functionality badges.

The conference was made possible by the hard work and cooperation of many people working in several different committees and organizations, all of which are listed in these proceedings. In particular, we are grateful to the PC members for their commitment and thorough reviews, and for their active participation in the discussion phase, and to all the external reviewers for their help in evaluating submissions. We are also grateful to the AEC members for their rigorous assessment of submitted artifacts and their reviews. Finally, we also thank the DisCoTec General Chair, Carla Ferreira, and the DAIS Steering Committee chair, Luís Veiga, for their constant availability, support, and guidance.

May 2023

Marta Patiño-Martínez
João Paulo

DAIS 2023 Organization

General Chair

Carla Ferreira   NOVA University Lisbon, Portugal

Program Committee Chairs

Marta Patino-Martínez   Technical University of Madrid, Spain
João Paulo   University of Minho and INESC TEC, Portugal

Steering Committee

Lydia Y. Chen   TU Delft, Netherlands
Frank Eliassen   University of Oslo, Norway
Rüdiger Kapitza   Technical University of Braunschweig, Germany
Rui Oliveira   University of Minho and INESC TEC, Portugal
Hans P. Reiser   University of Passau, Germany
Laura Ricci   University of Pisa, Italy
Silvia Bonomi   Università degli Studi di Roma "La Sapienza",
                                     Italy
Etienne Riviére   École Polytechnique de Louvain, Belgium
José Pereira   University of Minho and INESC TEC, Portugal
Luís Veiga (Chair)   INESC-ID, Universidade de Lisboa, Portugal

Program Committee

Ainhoa Azqueta   Universidad Politécnica de Madrid, Spain
Claudio Mezzina   University of Urbino, Italy
Daniel O'Keeffe   Royal Holloway, University of London, UK
Davide Frey   INRIA, France
Emanuel Onica   Alexandru Ioan Cuza University of Iasi, Romania
Evangelia Kalyvianaki   University of Cambridge, UK
Etienne Riviére   École Polytechnique de Louvain, Belgium
Fábio Coelho   University of Minho and INESC TEC, Portugal
Fábio Kon   University of São Paulo, Brazil

Hans P. Reiser   Reykjavík University, Iceland
Hein Meling   University of Stavanger, Norway
João Leitão   Universidade Nova de Lisboa, Portugal
Kostas Magoutis   University of Ioannina, Greece
Miguel Matos   IST INESC-ID, Universidade de Lisboa, Portugal
Pierre-Louis Aublin   IIJ Research Laboratory, Japan
Pierre Sutra   Télécom SudParis, France
Romain Rouvoy   University of Lille, France
Silvia Bonomi   Università degli Studi di Roma "La Sapienza",
                                      Italy
Spyros Voulgaris   Athens University of Economics and Business,
                                      Greece
Valerio Schiavoni   University of Neuchâtel, Switzerland
Vana Kalogeraki   Athens University of Economics and Business,
                                      Greece
Vincenzo Gulisano   Chalmers University, Sweden

Artefact Evaluation Committee Chairs

António Sousa   University of Minho and INESC TEC, Portugal
Vinícius Vielmo Cogo   Universidade de Lisboa, Portugal

Artefact Evaluation Committee

Bijun Li   Hainan Normal University, China
Cláudia Brito   University of Minho and INESC TEC, Portugal
Christian Berger   University of Passau, Germany
Giovanni Farina   Sapienza University of Rome, Italy
Nuno Dionísio   Universidade de Lisboa, Portugal
Robin Vassantlal   Universidade de Lisboa, Portugal
Tânia Esteves   University of Minho and INESC TEC, Portugal

Additional Reviewers

Adrien Luxey-Bitri   University of Lille, France
Bijun Li   Hainan Normal University, China
Christel Sirocchi   University of Urbino, Italy
Rémy Raes   INRIA, France
Thomas Dangl   University of Passau, Germany

Contents

Distributed Algorithms and Systems

TADA: A Toolkit for Approximate Distributed Agreement

Eduardo Lourenço da Conceição[1,2]($\boxtimes$) ⓘ, Ana Nunes Alonso[1,2] ⓘ,
Rui Carlos Oliveira[1,2] ⓘ, and José Orlando Pereira[1,2] ⓘ

[1] Universidade do Minho, Braga, Portugal
eduardo.l.conceicao@inesctec.pt
[2] INESC TEC, Braga, Portugal

Abstract. Approximate agreement has long been relegated to the side-lines compared to exact consensus, with its most notable application being clock synchronisation. Other proposed applications stemming from control theory target multi-agent consensus, namely for sensor stabilisation, coordination in robotics, and trust estimation. Several proposals for approximate agreement follow the Mean Subsequence Reduce approach, simply applying different functions at each phase. However, taking clock synchronisation as an example, applications do not fit neatly into the MSR model: Instead they require adapting the algorithms' internals.

Our contribution is two-fold. First, we identify additional configuration points, establishing a more general template of MSR approximate agreement algorithms. We then show how this allows us to implement not only generic algorithms but also those tailored for specific purposes (clock synchronisation). Second, we propose a toolkit for making approximate agreement practical, providing classical implementations as well as allow these to be configured for specific purposes. We validate the implementation with classical algorithms and clock synchronisation.

Keywords: approximate agreement · distributed systems primitives · practical toolkit · clock synchronisation

1 Introduction

In the realm of distributed systems, the problem of distributed agreement has been widely researched. Many solutions to this problem have been proposed over the years, in many different models, limited by the FLP Impossibility [18]: in an asynchronous system, no algorithm can guarantee termination in the case that one of the participants is faulty. Simply put, approximate distributed agreement, or approximate consensus, is defined as the problem of guaranteeing that correct processes decide on values with limited dispersion. Interestingly, solutions to approximate agreement are not bound by that impossibility. A more formal

Artifacts available in https://doi.org/10.5281/zenodo.7830167.

treatment of the approximate agreement problem is provided in Sect. 3. Approximate agreement was originally proposed with synchronous and asynchronous solutions [13] for a bounded number of Byzantine faults. Other proposals in the asynchronous model weaken adversaries, for example, by introducing communication primitives that guarantee FIFO order [8]. Adaptable protocols regarding synchrony conditions [20] or fault models [16] have also been proposed. Different sets of assumptions regarding fault detection have been considered, either by considering that faulty values can be uniformly detected [28], or refining resilience guarantees considering combined sets of fault classes [20,31]. Approximate agreement has narrower applicability than exact agreement as the nature of the operations performed in successive approximation rounds requires the convergent value (vote) to be numerical. Multi-dimensional versions of the problem have also been proposed [29]. These protocols have shown some promising applicability for clock synchronisation [14,24–28], sensor input stabilisation [34], distributed control [11] and trust estimation [33]. Still, approximate consensus has been mostly left in the realm of theory, while multiple frameworks and libraries have been made available for exact agreement (Sect. 2). In this work we: 1) provide TADA, a practical toolkit that makes data structures and primitives backed by approximate agreement available to Java developers through both blocking and non-blocking interfaces that encapsulate an algorithm's implementation (Sect. 5); 2) take advantage of some structural regularity in approximate agreement algorithms to create a template and thus simplify the implementation of further generic approximate agreement primitives, as well as of special-purpose protocols (Sects. 3 and 4); 3) validate the toolkit with the implementation of classical algorithms, and validate our approach and toolkit usability through the implementation of a clock synchronisation algorithm that exposes the clock value as an atomic variable (Sect. 6).

2   Related Work

Implementations of distributed agreement protocols have been made available to developers in two ways. One is through frameworks like Atomix [1], which encapsulate the agreement protocols and expose atomic data structures and primitives to the developer, or jgroups-raft [5], which implements the Raft protocol in JGroups [4], providing data structures and primitives such as leader election. TADA implements primitives that encapsulate approximate distributed agreement using a similar interface to the one found in Atomix distributed atomic variables. The other is to provide libraries such as libpaxos [32], a C implementation of Paxos [23]; etcd [3], a Go framework implementing the Raft protocol [7]; Bft-SMaRt [2] which implements a simple interface for state machine replication; MirBFT [6,35], a toolkit for implementing distributed algorithms. Babel [19], Appia [30] and Coyote [9] follow similar philosophies, implementing generic frameworks that can be used to build distributed algorithms, by providing the programmer with the necessary building blocks to construct distributed algorithms, with little abstraction. To the best of our knowledge, there are no generally-available frameworks or libraries providing implementations of approximate agreement protocols nor of its applications, including clock synchronisation. We highlight that TADA's approach, similar to Atomix's own, is singular in that it integrates with Java native concurrency mechanisms through `CompletableFuture`.

3   Approximate Distributed Agreement

A message passing system is said to be asynchronous if no assumptions, be they absolute or relative, are made regarding the time it takes to perform an action, namely to deliver or process a message. A synchronous system model imposes limits on clocks and message transmission and processing time. We define Byzantine processes as able to exhibit arbitrary behaviour which includes omitting messages, sending the same message to all processes with inaccurate values or sending messages to different processes with conflicting claims. Intuitively, the latter is the most challenging to tackle as it induces some asymmetry between processes.

The problem of approximate distributed agreement can be defined from that of exact distributed agreement by relaxing the agreement property and reframing integrity as validity [13]:

ϵ-**Agreement** All correct processes decide on values that differ by, at most, $\epsilon > 0$;
Validity If a correct process decides on a value v, v is within the range of the initial values of correct processes.
Termination All correct processes eventually decide.

While exact consensus has been proven to be impossible to solve in asynchronous systems with at least one faulty process [18], approximate agreement can be solved in asynchronous systems, tolerating at most t Byzantine processes in $n \geq 5t + 1$ total processes [13], while in a synchronous context, the minimum for n goes to $n \geq 3t + 1$. Although it has been proven that the resilience in the asynchronous model can, theoretically, be increased to match that of the synchronous model [17], such proposals introduce additional assumptions (e.g. a FIFO broadcast primitive [8]). Inexact consensus [28], or $(\epsilon, \delta, \gamma)$-agreement [17], is a variation on approximate agreement, such that the validity condition is relaxed:

γ-**Validity** If a correct process decides on a value v, v is in $[r_{min} - \gamma, r_{max} + \gamma]$, where r_{min} and r_{max} refer to the minimum and maximum values, respectively, of the initial values of correct processes.

δ is the precision of the multiset of votes (or amplitude, i.e. largest pairwise difference between values). Approximate agreement is equivalent to inexact agreement with $\gamma = 0$, meaning approximate agreement has tighter accuracy but looser precision [28].

3.1   Mean-Subsequence-Reduce (MSR)

Several proposed approximate agreement algorithms follow generically the same strategy, which defines the *Mean-Subsequence-Reduce* class [10,31]. MSR-class algorithms are round-based: in a given round h, each process p broadcasts its own value (vote) v_p^{h-1}, collects values received from other processes in a multiset V, and applies some approximation function on this set to calculate its vote v_p^h for the next round $(h + 1)$. If a termination condition is fulfilled, the process decides on the latest calculated value. The approximation function f can be defined as:

$$f_{\sigma,\alpha}(V) = mean[select_\sigma(reduce^\alpha(V)]$$

where $reduce^\alpha$ removes α extreme values from the multiset V, $select_\sigma$ selects σ values from the resulting multiset (e.g. by sampling) and $mean$ produces the value for the next round (or decision) from the selected values. Values σ and α tend to be related to the number of faults (or faulty processes) to be tolerated. It is required that each application of f reduces the amplitude of the interval defined by the values in the multiset.

Criteria for termination depend on the targeted precision (ϵ), which is used along with the values collected in the first round (V_0) to calculate the number of rounds (H) that guarantees the expected properties, i.e. that for any two processes p and q, the values decided by p, v_p' and q, v_q' differ by no more than ϵ. H will depend on the ratio between the amplitude of the interval defined by the initial values $(\delta(V_0))$ and ϵ, and the number of tolerated faulty processes t. A lower bound for these rounds is well known: to tolerate t Byzantine processes, at least $t+1$ rounds of communication are required [12]. Algorithm 1 follows the MSR strategy as outlined:

1. Starting with its initial vote v, each process waits to collect n initial values in a multiset (lines 2, 11–18); the number of rounds to execute is calculated, and the first approximation is calculated (lines 3, 4); if a value is not received from a process q, a default value is filled in (lines 15–16). This step is known as messageExchange.
2. In each round, each process sends its vote and waits for n votes, to then calculate the value for the next round (lines 5–7).
3. When the calculated number of rounds is reached, each process broadcasts its decision along with its final round number (lines 8–10).

The asynchronous version (see Algorithm 2), follows the same strategy, with the main change being that as timeouts can no longer be considered, in each message exchange, each process waits for $n - t$ votes (line 13), instead of n. The calculation of the number of rounds (line 3) and the approximation function (line 7) are adapted to handle the change in the size of the multiset, taking into consideration the change in resilience, from $n > 3t + 1$ to $n > 5t + 1$.

FCA (Algorithm 3) shares Algorithm 1's message exchange, with the main difference being the introduction of a predicate to filter out values considered not to be valid votes (line 21) and replacing them in the multiset with an estimate e_p required to be in the range of the values deemed acceptable A. As an example, the estimator function (line 6) can output the average, median or midpoint of the input multiset.

Finally, a word on algorithm selection. Because *Synch86* and *Async86* [13] serve as the basis over which many other proposals for approximate agreement

---

Algorithm 1: Synch86[13](SynchDLPSW86Instance.java)

Data: v

```
 1  Function InitializationRound:                    /* lines 159-212 */
 2  │   V₀ ← messageExchange (v,h);
 3  │   H ← ⌈log_c(n-2t,t)(δ(V₀)/ε)⌉;
 4  │   v₁ ← f_t,t(V₀);
 5  Function ApproximationRound:                      /* lines 214-271 */
 6  │   V_h ← messageExchange (v_{h-1},h);
 7  │   v_h ← f_t,t(V_h);
 8  Function TerminationRound:                        /* lines 279-283 */
 9  │   broadcast(<v_H,H>);
10  │   return v_H;
11  Function messageExchange(v, h):                   /* lines 457-472 */
12  │   broadcast(< v,h >);
13  │   while |V(h)| < n do
14  │   │   store v_q h in V_h
15  │   end
16  │   if q reaches timeout then           /* lines 176-197, 231-249 */
17  │   │   v_q h ← defaultValue;
18  │   end
19  │   return V_h;
```

---

are defined, we elected to analyze and implement these. The goal was two-fold: the barebones of the underlying structure should provide the foundation for a generic template for approximate agreement (see Sect. 4), for both synchronous and asynchronous models; and, by providing a modular implementation, it should facilitate the implementation of other algorithms through adaptation. *FCA* was selected for analysis and implementation for two reasons: its slightly different model as it was proposed to solve the inexact agreement problem [28], but which can nonetheless be converted to use the template defined in Sect. 4 for implementation; and it allows us to showcase the implementation of a clock synchronisation algorithm (Sect. 5), again taking full advantage of the modularity and adaptability of the template. The heterogeneity of the algorithms chosen become relevant in highlighting the similarities between different algorithms in order to better explain the template.

4   A Template for Approximate Agreement

Algorithms 1 and 3 have been adapted to better suit the more practical MSR model. In converting *Synch86* to Algorithm 1, as it is already very similar to *Async86*, the main change was to make explicit the initialization and termination rounds.

FCA was not originally defined as an iterative algorithm. However, since the rate of convergence is given, we can define a lower bound on the number of rounds needed to achieve ϵ-agreement (line 4 of Algorithm 3). However, the assumption of the existence of a function that can reliably determine whether received votes

---

Algorithm 2: Async86[13] (AsynchDLPSW86Instance.java)

Data: v

1 **Function** InitializationRound: /* lines 156-189 */
2   $\quad V_0 \leftarrow$ messageExchange (v,h);
3   $\quad H \leftarrow \lceil log_{c(n-3t,2t)}(\delta(V_0)/\epsilon)\rceil$;
4   $\quad v_1 \leftarrow mean(reduce^{2t}(V_0))$;
5 **Function** ApproximationRound: /* lines 191-226 */
6   $\quad V_h \leftarrow$ messageExchange (v_{h-1},h);
7   $\quad v_h \leftarrow f_{2t,t}(V_h)$;
8 **Function** TerminationRound: /* lines 234-239 */
9   $\quad$ broadcast($<v_H,H+1>$);
10 $\quad$ **return** v_H;
11 **Function** messageExchange $(v,\ h)$:   /* lines 406-420 */
12 $\quad$ broadcast($<v,h>$);
13 $\quad$ **while** $|V(h)| < n - t$ **do**
14 $\quad\quad$ | store $v_q h$ in V_h
15 $\quad$ **end**
16 $\quad$ **return** V_h;

---

are valid (line 5 in Algorithm 3) impacts the calculation of the number of rounds to execute. Parameter δ is to be calculated over the multiset of votes at round 0 from *correct* processes, which, for a generic implementation, would likely require a failure detector, such as the ones described in [21,22], or some mechanism to limit the set of possibly faulty votes. By considering any value as acceptable in round 0, we can emulate the correct behaviour of the algorithm, but it does mean that convergence will be slower, in case faulty processes cast votes that are arbitrarily distant from correct processes, and may produce results with looser accuracy, but that maintain the targeted precision. With these modifications to *FCA*, Algorithms 1, 2 and 3 have similar structures.

We can now abstract away from the specific details of each algorithm, to create a generic template for approximate agreement algorithms with sufficient configurability to implement multiple general approximate agreement algorithms as well as customize these for specific applications. Algorithm 4 presents the template, which allows implementations to provide the function used to calculate the number of rounds (rounds line 3), the approximation function (approximation lines 4, 7), a function to be executed whenever a message is received (onReceive line 13) and a function that defines whether the conditions for ending a message exchange have been met (endExchangeCondition line 12). It is assumed that these methods have access to parameters such as n, t, ϵ, etc., and that relevant state can be passed as needed. This is the case in the toolkit described in Sect. 5.

As an example, Algorithm 5 shows how to define the configurable functions to implement *Async86*. A few notes: 1) by default, no action is taken onReceive; 2) approximation receives the current round number (h) as an argument to allow round-specific behaviour to be defined; and 3) potential timeouts are simply ignored (line 17). Algorithm 6 shows how to implement *FCA* using the template.

Algorithm 3: Fast Convergence Algorithm (FCA)[28] (FCAInstance.java)

Data: v

1   **Function** `InitializationRound`:   /* lines 151-208 */
2      $V_0 \leftarrow$ `messageExchange` (v,h);
3      $\delta \leftarrow \delta(V_0)$;
4      $H \leftarrow log_{\frac{2}{3}}(\frac{\epsilon}{\delta})$;
5      $v_1 \leftarrow$ `approximation` (V_0, δ);
6   **Function** `ApproximationRound`:   /* lines 210-287 */
7      $V_h \leftarrow$ `messageExchange` (v_{h-1},h);
8      $v_1 \leftarrow$ `approximation` (V_0, δ);
9   **Function** `TerminationRound`:   /* lines 295-299 */
10     $broadcast(<v_H,H+1>)$;
11   **return** v_H;
12 **Function** `messageExchange`(v, h):   /* lines 447-462 */
13     $broadcast(<v,h>)$;
14   **while** $|V(h)| < (n)$ **do**
15 | store $v_q h$ in V_h
16   **end**
17   **if** q *reaches timeout* **then**   /* lines 170-196, 229-251 */
18 | $v_q h \leftarrow nil$
19   **end**
20   **return** V_h;
21 **Function** `approximation`(V, δ):
22     $A \leftarrow acceptable(V, \delta)$;
23     $e_p \leftarrow estimator(A)$;
24   **for** v_i *in* V *not in* A **do**
25 | $v_i \leftarrow e_p$;
26   **end**
27   **return** *mean(V)*;

---

5   How to Use the Toolkit

Our approach for providing a toolkit is based on frameworks such as Atomix [1] that provide primitives for building distributed applications. We provide primitives that encapsulate approximate agreement that are easy to incorporate into existing applications. The toolkit is implemented in the Java programming language. Communication uses Asynchronous Socket Channels from Java NIO.2 and is opaque to the programmer. The source code of the TADA toolkit is available as a GitHub repository (https://github.com/Tarly127/TADA). The `Processor` object keeps track of the group topology and integrates new processes into the group. In practise, this means keeping a record of all connections a trusted process has. For bootstrapping, processes connect to a trusted process, the broker, which is a static entity. Whenever a new process is added to the group, the list of connections the broker keeps is sent to the new member so it can connect to those same processes and a clique can be maintained. The correctness of the trusted process affects the integration process, not the correctness

---

Algorithm 4: MSR-based Template (ConsensusInstanceSkeleton.java)

Data: v

1 **Function** InitializationRound: /* lines 174-228 */
2 $\quad$ $V_0 \leftarrow$ messageExchange (v,h);
3 $\quad$ $H \leftarrow$ rounds (V_0);
4 $\quad$ $v_1 \leftarrow$ approximation $(V_0, v, 0)$;
5 **Function** ApproximationRound: /* lines 230-290 */
6 $\quad$ $V_h \leftarrow$ messageExchange (v_{h-1}, h);
7 $\quad$ $v_h \leftarrow$ approximation (V_h, v_{h-1}, h);
8 **Function** TerminationRound: /* lines 298-305 */
9 $\quad$ broadcast($<v_H, H+1>$); **return** v_H;
10 **Function** messageExchange(v, h):   /* lines 484-504 */
11 $\quad$ broadcast($<v,h>$);
12 $\quad$ **while** !endExchangeCondition (V_h, h) **do**
13 $\quad\quad$ store onReceive $(v_q h)$ in V_h;
14 $\quad\quad$ **if** q *reaches timeout* **then**   /* lines 192-212,247-266 */
15 $\quad\quad\quad$ $v_q h \leftarrow$ defaultValue;
16 $\quad\quad$ **end**
17 $\quad$ **end**
18 $\quad$ **return** (V_h);

---

of approximate consensus algorithms. While this is a strong assumption, this is a temporary measure, and the user of the toolkit may implement or integrate fault tolerant measures to create the communication group, using, for example, an `AtomixCluster`.

Listing 1.1 shows how simple it can be to use the toolkit. To create a `Processor`, one must instantiate it by passing it the address of the broker and its own address, each separated as the hostname and port. If no bootstrapping process exists, this `Processor` becomes so (line 1). The new `Processor` connects to the bootstrap process and, eventually, to the rest of the group. From a `Processor`, one can create an atomic primitive associated to the `Processor`'s group, which is defined as the set of `Processors` this `Processor` is connected to. In this example, the variable `atomicPrimitive` is instantiated to hold an `AtomicApproximateDouble` (lines 2, 3) which reading (line 5) or writing (line 6) can trigger approximate agreement instances among the `Processor`'s group. Parameters include a name such that primitive objects in different `Processors` with the same name are considered to be keeping track of the same distributed value, ϵ, and a timeout value and time unit, for synchronous algorithms, for example. The initial vote can also be defined on instantiation. In case the communication group that the `Processor` is connected to does not contain enough processes for the specific type of consensus algorithm to guarantee correctness, the instantiation method blocks until the required number of participants is reached. This number is based on the number of processes each algorithm requires to guarantee correctness. As of the writing of this document, the number is fixed.

Algorithm 5: Async implementation based on Algorithm 4

---

1 **Function** rounds(V_0):
2   **return** $\lceil log_{c(n-3t,2t)}(\delta(V_0)/\epsilon) \rceil$;
3 **Function** approximation(V_h, v^{h-1}, h):
4   **if** h *is* 0 **then**
5   **return** $mean(reduce^{2t}(V_0))$;
6   **end**
7   **else**
8   **return** $f_{2t,t}(V_h)$;
9   **end**
10 **Function** onReceive(v_q^h):
11   **return** v_{qh};
12 **Function** endExchangeCondition(V_h,h):
13   **return** $|V_h| \geq n - t$;

Listing 1.1. How to use the toolkit in JAVA

```java
var processor = new Processor("localhost","12345","localhost","12345");
var atomicPrimitive = processor.newAtomicApproximateDouble(
    "atomicPrimitive", 0.005, 1, TimeUnit.SECONDS);
atomicPrimitive.lazySet(1.5);
var newValue = atomicPrimitive.get();
var asyncAtomicPrimitive = processor.newAsyncAtomicApproximateDouble(
    "asyncAtomicPrimitive", 0.005);
CompletableFuture<Void> setRes = asyncAtomicPrimitive.set(3.0);
setRes.get();
var atomicPrimitiveTmp1 = processor.newAtomicApproximateDouble(
    "atomicPrimitive", 0.005, 1, TimeUnit.SECONDS,
    new ApproximateConsensusHandler<Void>{
        // method implementations go here
    });
```

An atomic variable can be updated with *eager* or *lazy* setters and getters. *Lazy* operations will only update or query the private internal value, i.e. the value available to the process at that time, while the *eager* operations will trigger approximate consensus algorithms on the value in the group. Other methods, such as compareAndSet, found in the atomic interface of the Java Standard Library, are also implemented. As an example, the lazySet in line 4 sets this Processor's vote for the value of variable atomicPrimitive to 1.5, in future approximate agreement instances. Another usage example of *lazy* methods can be found in the implementation of the faulty process in the FCA-based clock synchronisation case-study (see Sect. 6). The (*eager*) get in line 5 triggers an instance of approximate agreement on the value of that same variable. These methods can be blocking or non-blocking (with callbacks), which is not necessarily determined by the synchrony model of the selected approximate agreement algorithm. Non-blocking variants include Async in the method name (lines 6, 7). Querying with non-blocking methods returns a CompletableFuture, which

---

Algorithm 6: FCA implementation based on Algorithm 4

Data: δ

1   **Function** rounds(V_0):

2 | $\delta \leftarrow \delta(V_0)$;

3 | **return** $log_{\frac{2}{3}}(\frac{\epsilon}{\delta})$;

4   **Function** approximation(V_h, v_{h-1}, h):

5 | $A \leftarrow$ acceptable(V_h, δ);

6 | $e_p \leftarrow$ estimator(A);

7 | **for** v_i *in* V_h *not in* A **do**

8 | | $v_i \leftarrow e_p$;

9 | **end**

10 | **return** *mean(*V_h*)*;

11 **Function** onReceive(v_q^h):

12 | **return** v_q^h;

13 **Function** endExchangeCondition(V_h,h):

14 | **return** $|V_h| \geq n$;

---

will contain the result when it becomes available (lines 8, 9). Blocking methods default to *Synch86*, based on the template in Algorithm 4 and non-blocking methods default to *Async86*. An implementation of Algorithm 6 is also available.

5.1 Specifying Generic Primitive Variables

A generic primitive variable can be instantiated by additionally providing an implementation (lines 10–14 in Listing 1.1) of the `ApproximateConsensusHandler` interface (Listing 1.2). This interface specifies a method for each configurable function for the template defined in Sect. 4. Each method is provided with a `ConsensusState` object, with parameters such as n, t, ϵ, etc. A utility class `ConsensusAttachment` can be defined by the user, with additional parameters relevant for specific implementations of approximate consensus algorithms. Additionally, we provide a convenience method (lines 4–7) to allow processes to retrieve an up-to-date value for the vote, if necessary, just as a new consensus instance is starting, triggered by a different process.

To further illustrate how the toolkit can be used, a clock synchronisation algorithm based on *FCA* was implemented. Algorithm 7 shows how each configurable function was defined. Convergence is bounded in the same manner as Algorithm 6.

`clock()` is assumed to output the value of the process's perceived clock. The parameter λ is defined by the programmer as the expected amount of time it takes for a message to be delivered, once it has been sent, and is defined in and accessed through the `ConsensusAttachment` object. Parameter δ is part of the state of the handler. By using the toolkit and building on its implementation of Algorithm 6 it is easy to implement a different algorithm, while abstracting most of the what is required in terms of communication and control.

Listing 1.2. ApproximateConsensusHandler interface

```
1
2  public interface ApproximateConsensusHandler<ConsensusAttachment>
3  {
4      default Double onNewConsensus(final ConsensusState cs,
5                                    Double latestVote,
6                                    final ConsensusAttachment ca)
7      { return latestVote; }
8
9      default int rounds(final ConsensusState cs, double[] VO,
10                         final ConsensusAttachment ca)
11     { return Functions.SynchH(VO, cs.epsilon, cs.n, cs.t); }
12
13     default Double onReceive(final ConsensusState cs,
14                              ApproximationMessage msg,
15                              final ConsensusAttachment ca)
16     { return msg.v; }
17
18     default double approximationRound(final ConsensusState cs,
19                              double[] V, double v, int round,
20                              final ConsensusAttachment ca)
21     {
22         return (cs.H == null || round <= cs.H) ?
23             Functions.f(V, cs.t, cs.t) : v;
24     }
25
26     default boolean endExchangeCondition(final ConsensusState cs,
27                              double[] multiset, int round,
28                              final ConsensusAttachment ca)
29     { return multiset.length >= cs.n - 1; }
30 }
```

6   Evaluation

Our evaluation of the toolkit is two-fold: First, using known algorithms we validate that results obtained with the toolkit match the theoretical predictions. Then, we examine the performance that can be obtained using the toolkit, using clock synchronisation as a use case. The evaluation was conducted in a host with 48 physical cores, each an Intel®Xeon®Gold 6342. For each algorithm, 300 instances with the same set of initial values were run. Results from the initial 100 instances were discarded because these runs were significantly affected by Java's JIT compiler's harsher optimisations, which resulted in significant variability, especially when taking into consideration the fact that each individual instance of consensus lasts for a very small amount of time, in the range of milliseconds. For synchronous algorithms, the timeout value was adapted to the number of processes, increasing linearly with the number of processes. The rationale is that for the same number of threads in each processor, which does not change with n, processing the necessary messages for each round will be increasingly more costly. We defined the target precision (ϵ) to be 0.005, and the amplitude of the generated initial values to fall within $[0, 1)$.

Algorithm 7: FCA-based Clock Synchronisation implementation based on the template in Algorithm 4

Data: δ, λ

1 **Function** rounds(V_0):
2     $\delta \leftarrow \delta(V_0)$;
3   **return** $log_{\frac{2}{3}}(\frac{\epsilon}{\delta})$;
4 **Function** approximation(V_h, v_{h-1}, h):
5   **for** v_q^h *in* V_h **do**
6 | $v_q^h \leftarrow$ clock() $- v_q^h$;
7   **end**
8     $A \leftarrow$ acceptable(V_h, δ);
9     $e_p \leftarrow$ estimator(A);
10   **for** v_i *in* V_h *not in* A **do**
11 | $v_i \leftarrow e_p$;
12   **end**
13   **return** *mean(V_h)*;
14 **Function** onReceive(v_q^h):
15   **return** *clock()*$-\lambda v_q^h$;
16 **Function** endExchangeCondition(V_h,h):
17   **return** $|V_h| \geq n$;

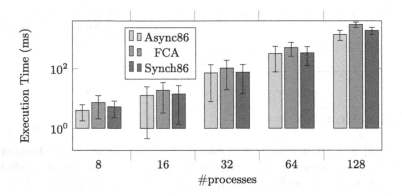

Fig. 1. Average decision time for n processes

Figure 1 shows how long it takes for processes to decide, on average. Without faults, *Async86* and *Synch86* outperform *FCA* consistently. This is to be expected, as both require a smaller number of rounds to achieve consensus than *FCA*, and the latter also performs more complex operations on each approximation round. Also, as the number of processes increases, *Async86* clearly starts to outperform *Synch86* significantly. Again this is consistent with theoretical predictions as the number of messages to be processed in each round with *Async86* is smaller than for *Synch86*: $n - t$ messages per round vs n, respectively.

Scalability also follows the expected pattern. Because we fixed the amplitude of the initial values, the number of necessary rounds (H) is a constant. Excluding

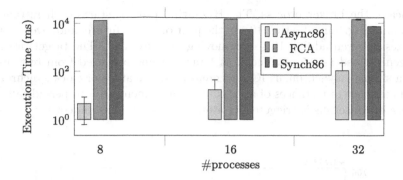

Fig. 2. Average and standard deviation of decision time for n processes with faults

its own vote, each process processes $n-1$ messages per round for the synchronous algorithms, and $n - t - 1$ messages per round for the asynchronous algorithm. The global overhead of message processing is proportional to $Hn^2 - Hn$ in synchronous algorithms, and $Hn^2 - Htn - Hn$ in the asynchronous algorithm. This means that, for both cases, when n is doubled, the number of messages needed is approximately quadrupled. For example, for *Async86*, average decision time for 128 processes (1394 ms) is approximately 4.25× larger than for 64 processes (318 s). In the case that the targeted precision tightens, the number of rounds will grow logarithmically.

Figure 2 shows the average decision time in the presence of faults. For each algorithm we considered the maximum tolerable number of Byzantine processes: $\lfloor (n-1)/3 \rfloor$ for *Synch86* and *FCA*; $\lfloor (n-1)/5 \rfloor$ for *Async86*. For each message, a Byzantine process has $1/3$ probability of omitting the message, or if not omitted, $1/3$ probability of sending a semantically incorrect message, i.e. a random value, resulting in a $5/9$ probability of a fault occurring. We observe that both *Synch86* and *FCA* take an order of magnitude longer to achieve consensus in the presence of faults than *Async86*. Again, this behaviour matches the theory. In the presence of a single omissive fault in a given round, in the synchronous algorithm, all processes will go into timeout in said round. Given that such a fault is propagated by at least one process in every round, all rounds will go into timeout. This does not happen in the case of *Async86*, as it does not wait for t processes, and no more than t omissive faults exist, functioning in the exact same way as it does in the absence of faults. Even so, *Synch86* performs consistently better than *FCA*, as it has less rounds.

We use clock synchronisation, one of the most well-known applications of approximate agreement, to demonstrate the flexibility of the toolkit for implementing new approximate agreement algorithms. To do so, the implementation of Algorithm 6 was converted to an implementation of Algorithm 7. Reading the value of the synchronised clock for an application is now as simple as invoking `get()` (line 5, Listing 1.1). Figure 3 shows the convergence of the algorithm when synchronising the clocks of 8 processes, one of which is Byzantine (in blue), specifically the broker process. The Byzantine process starts each instance of approximate agreement either 10 s in the past or in the future, and, every round, oscillates between adding 10 s or removing 10 s from v^h. The target precision has been defined as 0.5 ms, and λ as 1 ms, a value retrieved from test results using a simple Asynchronous IO benchmark. As a feature of clock synchronisation, a sequence of instances of approximate agreement are run periodically. An instance of consensus is triggered $1s$ after the last one has ended, for a total of 50 s.

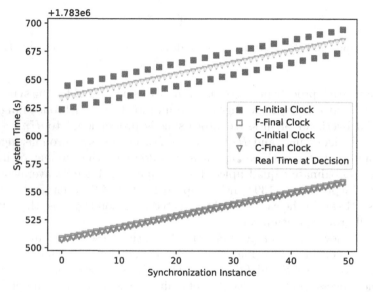

Fig. 3. FCA Clock Synchronisation Convergence with the presence of a faulty process

In Fig. 3, we can observe the initial values of correct clocks (marked with C) contrasted with the initial values of the faulty process (marked with F), and the clock values toward which both converged, as well as the real time at the point of decision. Clocks are indeed very close to each other at the end of each instance of re-synchronisation. Although not noticeable in the graph, the decided value in the faulty process is not within ϵ of correct processes. This is expected, as, while the algorithm guarantees that, if a process begins approximate agreement with a faulty vote, it will reach the target precision, such guarantee is not made when the same process propagates further semantic faults in every round, including to itself. Nonetheless, correct processes achieved the expected precision. However, they are all in the past, not only of the real clock at the end of execution, but also of the clock each processor had in the beginning, which can be observed from the discrepancy of about 125 s between the initial votes and the final clock values. This is due to the constant λ the algorithm required. This constant must be obtained through testing and is defined at the beginning of the program. As it is a theoretical measure of how long a process takes to receive, process and then respond to a message, at most. This highlights a problem in the definition of the system assumptions, as this constant can affect the algorithm's accuracy. No proper way to define this value is provided in the original literature, and modelling synchronous constants in asynchronous environments is tricky. Nevertheless, correctness, by definition of FCA, was achieved, as all correct processes reached agreement on a value within the defined precision. Other Byzantine behaviours such as consistently sending votes 10s in the future were tested and results were very similar to those already presented.

7 Conclusion

We propose a toolkit that makes approximate agreement algorithms easier to use in practical settings and foster the implementation of new algorithms or their adaptation for specific purposes by reusing as much code as possible. We analysed several algorithms, namely some in the MSR class (or thus converted), to generate a template and well-defined configuration points to support. Results showed that the template-based implementation, both synchronous and asynchronous, match the theoretically predicted behaviour in terms of decision latency and resilience. We implemented a clock synchronisation algorithm as an adaptation of a classical algorithm (FCA), exposing the clock variable as an atomic variable, just by providing implementations for the chosen configuration points, via AsynchronousConsensusHandler interface. Results showed the implementation behaved as expected, even in the presence of a Byzantine process. Using this generic template in the future, we hope that others may use the toolkit to stabilise inputs from sensors, in ad hoc mobile networks [26], or distributed machine learning [15].

References

1. Atomix: A reactive java framework for building fault-tolerant distributed systems. https://atomix.io/
2. Bft-smart: High-performance byzantine fault-tolerant state machine replication. http://bft-smart.github.io/library/
3. etcd: A distributed, reliable key-value store for the most critical data of a distributed system. https://etcd.io/
4. Jgroups - a toolkit for reliable messaging. http://www.jgroups.org/
5. jgroups-raft: Implementation of the raft consensus protocol in jgroups. http://belaban.github.io/jgroups-raft/
6. Mirbft. https://labs.hyperledger.org/labs/mir-bft.html
7. The Raft consensus algorithm. https://raft.github.io/
8. Abraham, I., Amit, Y., Dolev, D.: Optimal resilience asynchronous approximate agreement. In: International Conference on Principles of Distributed Systems, pp. 229–239 (2005). https://doi.org/10.1007/11516798_17
9. Bhatti, N.T., Hiltunen, M.A., Schlichting, R.D., Chiu, W.: Coyote: a system for constructing fine-grain configurable communication services. ACM Trans. Comput. Syst. **16**(4), 321–366 (1998). https://doi.org/10.1145/292523.292524

10. Bonomi, S., Pozzo, A.D., Potop-Butucaru, M., Tixeuil, S.: Approximate agreement under mobile byzantine faults. Theoret. Comput. Sci. **758**, 17–29 (2019). https://doi.org/10.1016/j.tcs.2018.08.001
11. Cady, S.T., Domínguez-García, A.D., Hadjicostis, C.N.: Finite-time approximate consensus and its application to distributed frequency regulation in islanded ac microgrids. In: 2015 48th Hawaii International Conference on System Sciences, pp. 2664–2670. IEEE (2015)
12. Dolev, D., Strong, H.R.: Authenticated algorithms for byzantine agreement. SIAM J. Comput. **12**(4), 656–666 (1983). https://doi.org/10.1137/0212045
13. Dolev, D., Lynch, N., Pinter, S., Stark, E., Wheil, W.: Reaching approximate agreement in the presence of faults. J. ACM **33**(3), 499–516 (1986). https://doi.org/10.1145/5925.5931
14. Dolev, S., Welch, J.L.: Self-stabilizing clock synchronization in the presence of byzantine faults. J. ACM **51**(5), 780–799 (2004). https://doi.org/10.1145/1017460.1017463
15. El-Mhamdi, E.M., Guerraoui, R., Guirguis, A., Rouault, S.: Garfield: system support for byzantine machine learning. arXiv preprint arXiv:2010.05888 (2020)
16. Fekete, A.D.: Asymptotically optimal algorithms for approximate agreement. Distrib. Comput. **4**, 9–29 (1990). https://doi.org/10.1007/BF01783662
17. Fischer, M.J., Lynch, N.A., Merrit, M.: Easy impossibility proofs for distributed consensus problems. Distrib. Comput. **2**, 26–39 (1986). https://doi.org/10.1007/BF01843568
18. Fischer, M.J., Lynch, N.A., Paterson, M.S.: Impossibility of distributed consensus with one faulty process. J. ACM **32**(2), 374–382 (1985). https://doi.org/10.1145/3149.214121
19. Fouto, P., Costa, P.A., Preguiça, N., Leitão, J.: Babel: a framework for developing performant and dependable distributed protocols. In: 2022 41st International Symposium on Reliable Distributed Systems (SRDS), pp. 146–155 (2022). https://doi.org/10.1109/SRDS55811.2022.00022
20. Ghinea, D., Liu-Zhang, C.D., Wattenhofer, R.: Optimal synchronous approximate agreement with asynchronous fallback. In: Proceedings of the 2022 ACM Symposium on Principles of Distributed Computing, pp. 70–80 (2022)
21. Haeberlen, A., Kouznetsov, P., Druschel, P.: The case for byzantine fault detection. In: HotDep (2006)
22. Kihlstrom, K.P., Moser, L.E., Melliar-Smith, P.M.: Byzantine fault detectors for solving consensus. Comput. J. **46**(1), 16–35 (2003). https://doi.org/10.1093/comjnl/46.1.16
23. Lamport, L.: Paxos made simple. ACM SIGACT News (Distributed Computing Column) 32, 4 (Whole Number 121, December 2001), pp. 51–58 (2001)
24. Lamport, L., Melliar-Smith, P.M.: Byzantine clock synchronization. In: Proceedings of the Third Annual ACM Symposium on Principles of Distributed Computing, PODC 1984, pp. 68–74. Association for Computing Machinery, New York (1984). https://doi.org/10.1145/800222.806737
25. Leidenfrost, R., Elmenreich, W., Bettstetter, C.: Fault-tolerant averaging for self-organizing synchronization in wireless ad hoc networks. In: 2010 7th International Symposium on Wireless Communication Systems, pp. 721–725 (2010). https://doi.org/10.1109/ISWCS.2010.5624283
26. Li, C., Wang, Y., Hurfin, M.: Clock synchronization in mobile ad hoc networks based on an iterative approximate byzantine consensus protocol. In: 2014 IEEE 28th International Conference on Advanced Information Networking and Applications (2014)

27. Lundelius, J., Lynch, N.: A new fault-tolerant algorithm for clock synchronization. In: Proceedings of the Third Annual ACM Symposium on Principles of Distributed Computing, PODC 1984, pp. 75–88. Association for Computing Machinery, New York (1984). https://doi.org/10.1145/800222.806738
28. Mahaney, S.R., Schneider, F.B.: Inexact agreement: accuracy, precision, and graceful degradation (1985). https://doi.org/10.1145/323596.323618
29. Mendes, H., Herlihy, M.: Multidimensional approximate agreement in byzantine asynchronous systems. In: Proceedings of the Forty-Fifth Annual ACM Symposium on Theory of Computing, STOC 2013, pp. 391–400. Association for Computing Machinery, New York (2013). https://doi.org/10.1145/2488608.2488657
30. Miranda, H., Pinto, A., Rodrigues, L.: Appia, a flexible protocol kernel supporting multiple coordinated channels. In: Proceedings 21st International Conference on Distributed Computing Systems, pp. 707–710 (2001). https://doi.org/10.1109/ICDSC.2001.919005
31. Plunkett, R., Fekete, A.: Approximate agreement with mixed mode faults: algorithm and lower bound. In: Kutten, S. (ed.) DISC 1998. LNCS, vol. 1499, pp. 333–346. Springer, Heidelberg (1998). https://doi.org/10.1007/BFb0056493
32. Primi, M., Sciascia, D.: Libpaxos: an open-source paxos. http://libpaxos.sourceforge.net/
33. Raghu Vamsi Krishna, T., Barnwal, R.P., Ghosh, S.K.: Cat: consensus-assisted trust estimation of MDS-equipped collaborators in vehicular ad-hoc network. Veh. Commun. 2(3), 150–157 (2015). https://doi.org/10.1016/j.vehcom.2015.06.001
34. Sadikhov, T., Haddad, W.M., Yucelen, T., Goebel, R.: Approximate consensus of multiagent systems with inaccurate sensor measurements. J. Dyn. Syst. Meas. Contr. 139(9), 091003 (2017)
35. Stathakopoulou, C., David, T., Vukolic, M.: Mir-BFT: high-throughput BFT for blockchains. CoRR abs/1906.05552 (2019). http://arxiv.org/abs/1906.05552

Studying the Workload of a Fully Decentralized Web3 System: IPFS

Pedro Ákos Costa[1]([✉]), João Leitão[1], and Yannis Psaras[2]

[1] NOVALINCS & NOVA University of Lisbon, Lisbon, Portugal
pah.costa@campus.fct.unl.pt, jc.leitao@fct.unl.pt
[2] Protocol Labs, San Francisco, USA
yiannis@protocol.ai

Abstract. In this paper we present a study of the workload of the Inter-Planetary File System (IPFS), a decentralized file system which is a key enabler of Web3. Our study focuses on the access patterns observed from one of the most popular IPFS gateways located in North America, and analyzes these access patterns in light of one of the most common assumptions made in regard to the access pattern of decentralized content sharing systems: that the access patterns are mostly geographically localized. However, through our study, we show that the access patterns are content-dependent rather than geographically localized. In our study, we found that access patterns mostly target a small set of popular content, which is provided by nodes in the North American and European regions, despite the location of the requester. Furthermore, we found that, interestingly, this popular content is only provided by a few nodes in the system, suggesting a significant imbalance both in content providers and in the access patterns of the system to the content. This in turn suggests that the system is significantly centralized on these few node providers.

Keywords: Web3 · Distributed Systems · Measurements

1 Introduction

The Internet nowadays is supported mostly by a few large cloud providers that include Google, Amazon, Microsoft, and Cloudflare. These providers host a wide variety of web services that operate at a large scale serving a huge number of users scattered throughout the World. Nevertheless, this paradigm forces application providers to fully rely and trust on the operators of these centralized cloud infrastructure, which dictate the terms of service with little to no competition.

This work was partially supported by FCT/MCTES grant SFRH/BD/144023/2019 and by the European Union's Horizon Europe Research and Innovation Programme under Grant Agreement No 101093006. Artifacts available in https://doi.org/10.5281/zenodo.7850384.

M. Patiño-Martínez and J. Paulo (Eds.): DAIS 2023, LNCS 13909, pp. 20–36, 2023.
https://doi.org/10.1007/978-3-031-35260-7_2

Moreover, in most application scenarios using cloud infrastructures the control of user data is relinquished, in some way, to these operators, which is undesirable (and being target of legislation such as the European GDPR), specially if we consider the susceptibility of attacks to cloud infrastructures [12,18]. To address this, and partially motivated by the increased popularity and use cases enabled by blockchain technologies [27,36], the concept of Web3 [16] has emerged. Web3 aims at decentralizing web technologies to improve user security and privacy as well as providing guaranteed ownership of user data, through the use of a combination of existing and novel peer-to-peer protocols [20,32].

However, Web3 is still in its early stages and has yet to become competitive with modern cloud infrastructures, in terms of flexibility, application development, security/privacy, and performance. This is due to the current Web3 main technology enablers: blockchain, that maintains and replicates the system state; libp2p [30], that is used to develop decentralized applications (dApps) and their support; and IPFS [3,34], that is used as an entry-point to most dApps, that are still restricted to the domains of content creation and sharing [10,28], decentralized financing [35], decentralized communication [4,9], among a few others. This is because, blockchain, although important for decentralization, also limits the amount of interactions applications can have, as these are mostly made through the replicated state machine materialized by blockchains, which have limited throughput. Furthermore, IPFS still has a large space for performance improvement, as recent studies show that searching for content on IPFS can take up to $2,5$ hours [5].

IPFS relies on a distributed hash table (DHT) to make content available to users in the network. The DHT organizes nodes and content according to a uniform distribution of identifiers that are assigned both to nodes and content. This however, leads the topology of the DHT to not match the physical network topology, which can cause routing to be performed across large distances for content that is published near the requesters. This is commonly known as the topology mismatch problem [21–23]. To address this issue, there are a number of works in the literature [1,7,13,17,26,31] that try to optimize and scale DHT designs by assuming that content access patterns presents a high level of locality, meaning that content is mostly accessed by users located in the (geographical) vicinity of users that published it.

In this paper we present an in-depth analysis of the workload on IPFS to verify if IPFS can benefit from such approaches that optimize for locality of content access. To this end, we have gathered two weeks worth of logs from one of the most popular IPFS gateways located in North America. These logs contained the (access) requests made from IPFS users across the World to large amounts of content stored in IPFS. We analyzed these logs and performed the same (valid) requests that were observed in the logs to fetch the information regarding the providers of the content.

While one of the contributions of this paper is the presentation of the novel methodology that we developed to be able to study the logs of a large-scale peer-to-peer system regarding its workload, our study allows us to make two additional contributions. First, to correlate the amount of content that is being provided on IPFS by different peers (providers) considering content that was requested through one of the most popular public IPFS gateways. Second, and through the use of the MaxMind [24] database that matches IP addresses to geolocation information, to identify the relation between the location of the origin of requests and location of providers of the requested content. With this data, we analyzed the IPFS workload and found that most content is provided only by a few providers that are mostly located on North America and Europe, and disprove the locality assumption commonly made in many peer-to-peer systems [1, 13].

The remainder of the paper is structured as follows: Sect. 2 provides a brief description of IPFS and how it operates. In Sect. 3 we detail our methodology to gather and analyze data used in this study. Section 4 presents our results, providing insights on the workload of the IPFS network. Section 5 discusses related work, and finally, Sect. 6 concludes the paper with final remarks and observations regarding the obtained results.

2 IPFS

IPFS is a large scale peer-to-peer distributed system that aims at connecting computing devices offering a shared file system. To enable this, IPFS relies on libp2p [30] to handle networking aspects. To provide a membership and lookup service among peers in the network, libp2p relies on a distributed hash table (DHT), implemented as a variant of the Kademlia protocol [25]. IPFS leverages this DHT to distribute and search content and locate peers in the system. Content in IPFS is immutable, with each individual piece of content (e.g., file, data block, etc.) being associated with an identifier (*CID*), that is a collection of hashes referred as a *multi-hash*, that includes the hash of the content and hashes of metadata describing the hashing mechanism. Similarly, each peer in IPFS also has an identifier (*peerId*) that is a multi-hash of the peer's public key. Peers organize themselves in the DHT according to a SHA-256 hash of their peerId and store content pointers according to the SHA-256 hash of the CID. Furthermore, each peer has associated to it a list of multi-addresses, that describe the Internet addresses of the peer (this can be ipv4, ipv6, and the transport protocols supported by that peer and ports).

IPFS peers do not store the content itself but only a pointer to the peer providing the content (the one that published the content). As such, for a peer to publish content on IPFS, the peer effectively announces to the network that it provides the content by storing in the IPFS DHT a *provider record*. A provider record contains a mapping of a CID to peerIds, i.e., the content providers. As per the Kademlia operation, this provider record will be stored in the k closest peers to the hash of the CID on the DHT. In IPFS k has a value of 20. Note that the same content can be provided by multiple peers.

To fetch content, IPFS uses a protocol named *Bitswap* [8] that performs both discovery and data transfer. For Bitswap to discover content it begins to perform a local one-hop flood request for the CID. This will send a message to all neighboring peers asking if they have the contents of the CID locally. Note that this process is highly optimistic as Bitswap leverages the fact that an IPFS node is connected to hundreds of other nodes (which are the nodes managed by

DHT protocol and cached nodes that were used in previous DHT searches). If the answer is positive, Bitswap begins transferring the content with a process akin to BitTorrent [11]. If the response is negative and the content cannot be found in a neighboring peer, it resorts to the DHT to find the provider records of the CID. Once Bitswap has obtained one provider record, it will start to try to transfer the content from providers indicated in that record.

IPFS has two modes of operation: as a server or as a client node. Server nodes are (usually) publicly reachable in the Internet and participate actively in the DHT to enable routing among peers and serve content to the network. Client nodes connect to the DHT, but do not maintain the DHT, meaning that client nodes can only perform requests to the DHT and do not participate in the routing process. Additionally, an IPFS peer acting as server can also act as an HTTP gateway. In this case the IPFS node also runs a web server that grants access to IPFS via a browser interface to users. In more detail, a gateway node is able to transform an HTTP request into a valid IPFS request, that will either trigger a Bitswap and/or DHT operation, allowing to serve the content to clients that are not running an IPFS node, and instead access to content via their browsers.

As it is common in many P2P systems, not all IPFS nodes are publicly reachable. This is the case for nodes that are behind a NAT. In this case, an IPFS node can request a publicly reachable IPFS node to relay traffic for itself. Furthermore, IPFS hosts third-party pinning services that host content for users on IPFS servers controlled by the pinning service provider for a fee.

3   Methodology

In this section we provide a detailed description of our methodology to study and characterize the IPFS workload. In summary, we collected two weeks worth (from March 7th to March 21st of 2022) of logs [6] from one of the most popular IPFS gateway – *ipfs.io* – that is located in North America. These logs were produced by a NGINX reverse proxy that logged every HTTP request made. Each entry in the log contains information about an HTTP request made by a user to that IPFS gateway.

To process these logs, we filtered all non-valid HTTP requests (e.g., POST operations and out of format entries), and extracted the CID in each valid HTTP request. From this filtered subset, we resorted to IPFS to obtain all the available provider records for each CID. To obtain geolocation information from both the requests and providers, we matched the IP addresses in the gateway logs and the provider record respectively against the MaxMind GeoLite2 Free Geolocation Database [24]. Note that, the dataset provided was anonymized by replacing the IP address of requesters with an identifier that maps to the geographic location of the requester.

Finally, we combined both datasets on the requested and provided CID to produce a global view that shows where content is requested and where that content was being served from. In the following, we describe this process in more detail.

3.1 Processing the Requests

The first step in analyzing the IPFS workload is to extract the requested CIDs. To do this, we parsed the gateway logs into a structured data format that can be easily processed. The gateway logs are generated by an NGINX reverse proxy, that serves as a frontend for an IPFS server node that acts as the IPFS gateway. Each log entry contains information about the received HTTP requests by the IPFS gateway. In particular, we are interested in the following information of the HTTP requests: the IP address of the requester, to extract geolocation information; the HTTP operation and the HTTP status, to filter unwanted HTTP requests for our study (e.g., POST operations and GET operations whose answer was had a 400 HTTP status); and the HTTP target and the HTTP host, that effectively contain the requested CID. In total the logs we collected contained 123,959,912 requests.

We begin by filtering logs that are out of format. This amounts to 0.001% of all requests and include requests that have unparseable HTTP targets which contained hexadecimal codes in that field. Next, we remove all requests that are not GET HTTP requests, as only GET requests actually make requests to IPFS (either through BitSwap or the DHT). This removed about 19% of all requests contained in the logs, leaving almost 81% of log entries with only GET operations.

However, not all GET operations are of interest to study the workload. Such is the case for GET operations that did not succeed (i.e., where the reply had an HTTP status code of 400) or that do not contain a CID in their request. We filter GET operations that did not succeed due to these having a high probability that the content is either invalid (i.e., it was never available on IPFS) or the content was no longer available at the time of the request. As for the CIDs in requests, these appear in the full `url` of the request that is obtained by concatenating the HTTP host field with the HTTP target field. Note that the HTTP host in this case can be `ipfs.io` (i.e., the gateway host), in which case the CID will appear on the HTTP target; or can be in the form of `<CID>.ipfs.dweb.link`, in which case the CID is in the HTTP host part. Note as well, these `url` contain a file system path to the requested content, which means that the CID might represent a folder containing multiple files. In the case a `url` contains multiple CIDs, we only consider the first CID, as effectively the gateway will only search for the first CID in the `url`, as the remaining accessed content can be found below the first CID in the (remote) file system path.

With this step, we filter out 41% of all GET operations, where 17% of these were GET operations that did not succeed and 24% were requests that did not contain a CID. With this, 47% of the total requests remained as valid GET operations, which were the ones consider in our study. Table 1 summarizes the number of requests we processed in each step for our study described above.

3.2 Locating the Content Providers

The second step in studying and characterizing the IPFS workload is to gather information on the providers of the requested content, as to understand where and by how many peers is the content served. To achieve this, we developed

Table 1. Requests processed summary.

	Number of entries	Percentage
Total	123, 959, 912	100%
Out of Format	2, 165	0.001%
Not GETs	24, 298, 396	19.602%
All GETs	82, 439, 744	80.396%
Valid GETs	58, 869, 788	47.491%

Table 2. Providers processed summary.

	Number of entries	Percentage
Total CIDs	4, 009, 575	100%
CIDs w/out provider	2, 175, 608	54.26%
CIDs w/ provider	1, 833, 967	45.74%
Providers	55, 830	100%
Providers w/out address	32, 968	59%
Providers w/ address	22, 862	41%
Providers w/ address after find	26, 886	48%

a simple libp2p application that connects to IPFS and requests all provider records for a given CID. Our application leverages the fact that IPFS uses the same networking software stack and DHT provided by libp2p (which by default connects to the IPFS network), to execute FINDPROVIDERS API calls to libp2p DHT to gather information for all providers of CIDs.

Out of the 58, 869, 788 valid GET operations, a total of 4, 009, 575 different CIDs were requested. We requested the providers of all these CIDs through our libp2p application. We found we were unable to locate the providers of 54% of all CIDs. This can be due to the fact that the content was no longer available on the network. Note that this study was perform about 6 months after the requests were recorded by the gateway. This enables us to focus our study on non-ephemeral content on IPFS which we argue is more representative of the workload of the system. From the CIDs with providers we discovered 55, 830 different providers however, 59% of these did not have any addressing information associated to them. This means that the peers storing the provider record did not receive any update on the provider (from any kind of traffic) for a window of time longer than 30 minutes, as such, the peers storing the provider record assumed the provider might have moved and changed its network address, thus deleting the previously known provider multi-address. To fetch the multi-address in these cases, we queried the DHT for the multi-address of the provider, and managed to find the multi-address of 4, 024 more providers (an additional 7% of providers regarding those obtained directly from provider records). Table 2 summarizes the numbers of processed CIDs and found providers.

3.3 Analyzing the Data

The final step to study and characterize the IPFS workload is to join both request and providers data to map from where in the World are requests being performed and where in the World is the content provided/available. This required us to extract geo-locality data from the gathered data. To this end, we use the Max-Mind GeoLite2 Free Geolocation Database [24], that provides the geolocation of a vast collection of public IP addresses. However, this database is not complete and may have IP addresses whose geolocation is unknown. Fortunately, for the request data all IP addresses had geolocation information. On the other hand, only 88% of providers with addresses had geolocation information.

Note that a provider is identified by a peerId and has multiple multi-addresses. To get the geolocation information of a provider we had to extract the (public) IP address of multi-addresses. For multi-addresses that contained protocols `ip4` and `ip6` this procedure is straightforward. This amounts to 98% all observed multi-address (excluding local address, such as `127.0.0.1` and `::1`); 0.6% of multi-addresses were DNS addresses, that we resolved with local DNS resolvers; and the remainder 1.4% of multi-address were relay multi-addresses, and hence the provider did not have a public reachable IP address, which we ignored in this study. For providers that had multiple locations (probably due to the use of VPN services), we considered the last observed location. These were just a few cases that do not impact significantly our study.

We have inserted both datasets into a PostgreSQL database for ease of analysis. This database has 2 tables, one containing the requests and another containing the providers. The requests table stores a request identifier (reqId), the timestamp the request was originally made to the gateway, the CID requested, and the location information of the requester. The requests table has as key the reqId, that is a hash of the request log entry, to avoid processing duplicate request entries from the log. The providers table stores: the CID provided, the peerId of the provider, and the location information of the provider. The provider table has as key the CID and peerId. This uniquely identifies each provider entry, since each CID can have multiple providers, and a provider can provide multiple CIDs. Notice that the CID in the providers table is a foreign key of the CID in the requests table.

By performing a join over the requests and providers table we can compute a mapping from where requests are performed to where they are provided. Before presenting the results in the next section, we follow by providing some implementation details on the mechanisms we employed to process and find content providers information.

3.4   Implementation Details

The code and scripts that were used to process the data for this study can be found in https://github.com/pedroAkos/IPFS-location-requested-content. The processing of data required fine-tuning of the parallelization of queries to IPFS. This was required because IPFS can take some time to retrieve the provider records from the DHT; from our study the average latency was about 6 seconds, with the maximum latency reaching 1.5 hours; we made parallel queries to IPFS to fetch provider records. However, libp2p can be extremely taxing on the network, as a libp2p node can maintain hundreds, or even thousands, of connections and perform thousands of requests. To put this in perspective, a process executing 100 queries in parallel to find providers would produce almost 10,000 packets per minute. The process to resolve all 4,009,575 distinct CIDs took approximately 40 hours.

4   Results

In this section we analyze the results from our study to understand if IPFS would benefit from a DHT design that assumes requests to have geographic locality. By doing so, our analysis aims to answer the following questions:

1. *How many requests are made to IPFS on average per day?*
2. *How is the request frequency distributed over different CIDs in the system?*
3. *How are providers geo-distributed in the system?*
4. *How is provided content distributed across providers in the system?*
5. *How does the location of requested content correlate with the location of providers for requested content?*

To answer these question, we analyze the data first from the point of view of requests by considering the requests data extracted from the gateway logs (Section. 4.1). We then analyze the data from the point of view of providers using the data we extracted directly from IPFS (Sect. 4.2). Finally, we combine information from both requests and providers data to produce a correlation between the location of requests' origins and content providers (Sect. 4.3).

4.1   Requests

In this section we analyze the results from the perspective of content fetchers. With this, we aim to answer the first two questions of our analysis. *How many requests are made to IPFS on average per day?* and *How is the request frequency distributed over different CIDs in the system?* We begin by answering the first question.

Figure 1 represents the client requests processed by the gateway per hour. Notice that Fig. 1a captures all requests made during the period of two weeks (x-axis), Fig. 1b captures the same requests but characterized by continent, and Figs. 1c and 1d focuses on the request traffic for the two regions with most traffic, North America (Fig. 1c and Asia (Fig. 1d), for only the first 3 days of the analysis period, with the night hours shaded on timezones that align with each region (GMT-7 and GMT+8 respectively).

Figure 1a shows that, on average, more than 150,000 requests per hour are made to the IPFS gateway, reaching a maximum of almost 275,000 requests per hour. Notice that on day 2022-03-14 the requests suddenly drop. We verified this, and indeed the logs we have from that day abruptly stop after a few hours (just before the 5 hour mark). Most likely, this was due to an issue with the gateway that day that made it unreachable for about 9 hours, which after then resumed processing requests regularly.

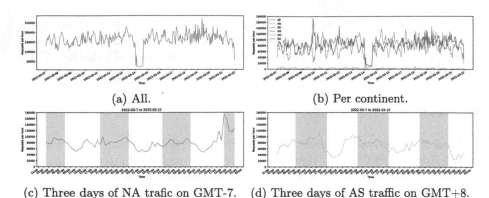

(a) All.

(b) Per continent.

(c) Three days of NA trafic on GMT-7.   (d) Three days of AS traffic on GMT+8.

Fig. 1. Requests over time.

From Fig. 1b we can see that most of the gateway traffic is split from North America (NA) and Asia (AS) with more than an average of 75, 000 requests per hour with origin on each region. The third region with the most requests per hour is Oceania (OC) with an average of around 2, 500 requests per hour. This is followed by Europe (EU) with an average of around 85 requests per hour, Africa (AF) with an average of around 57 requests per hour, and South America (SA) with an average of only 3 requests per hour. From these results we conclude that this IPFS gateway handles predominantly traffic from North America and Asia with a high volume of requests. Note that `ipfs.io` has an anycast DNS record [34], which means that there are multiple instance of the gateway located in the world (most likely there is an instance in Europe that handles the European traffic). Nevertheless, we argue that we have sufficient data to analyze if there is geographic locality in requested content.

To understand if this high volume of traffic has a day/night pattern, on Figs. 1c and 1d we plot the requests per day of the first 3 days of our analysis, and shaded the areas of the plot that represent the night cycle (between 21h and 7h). In Fig. 1c we plot the North American traffic and shaded the night hours on the gateway's timezone (GMT-7), and in Fig. 1d we plot the Asian traffic and shaded the night hours on the Asian timezone (GMT+8). From these results, there appears to be no obvious day/night pattern for the North American and Asian traffics. However, there is a slight tendency towards having more traffic during the night, although marginal. From these results we conclude that the IPFS gateway has a steady high volume of traffic that is not driven by geographical region nor by day/night cycles.

Figures 2 and 3 represent the frequency of requests performed for a CID (i.e., how many times was a CID requested from the gateway by a user). These results serve to answer question #2: *How is the request frequency distributed over different CIDs in the system?*

Figure 2a shows an Empirical CDF (ECDF) for all requested CIDs. Notice that the x-axis (representing the frequency of requests) is in logarithmic scale. The y-axis captures the proportion of requested CIDs with at most that amount of

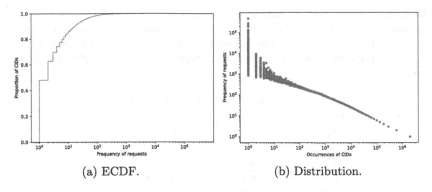

(a) ECDF.   (b) Distribution.

Fig. 2. All requested CIDs frequency.

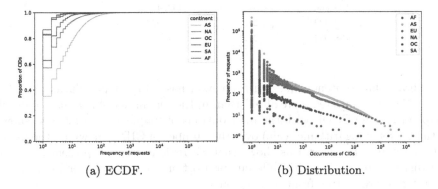

(a) ECDF.   (b) Distribution.

Fig. 3. Per continent requested CIDs frequency.

accesses. We notice that almost half of all CIDs are only requested once. After that, the frequency increases with decreasing increments on the proportion of CIDs, where about 90% of all CIDs are requested at most 10 times and about 99% of all CIDs are requested at most 100 times. Figure 2b complements the ECDF showing the distributions of frequency of requests (shown on the y-axis) over the number of CIDs (shown on the x-axis). Each point in this distribution represents how many CIDs where requested how many times. Note that both axis of this figure are in logarithmic scale. From this figure we can see the tendency on the frequency of requests over the number of CIDs, which resembles a typical Zipf distribution. Table 3 summarizes the frequency of the top 10 requested CIDs. We can further add, that most of these top 10 most requested CIDs were Non-Fungible Tokens (NFT) related data, suggesting that this is a primary use case for IPFS.

Figure 3 shows the same information but characterized by the following regions: Africa (AF), Asia (AS), Europe (EU), North America (NA), Oceania (OC), and South America (SA). Figure 3a shows an ECDF for the frequency of requested CIDs (on the x-axis in logarithmic scale) over the proportion of requests (on the y-axis), discriminated by region. We notice that almost 60% of requests originating from Asia, request at most the same CID thrice, whereas 60% of requests originating from North America request the same CID only once.

Table 3. Top 10 summary of data in descending order. The first column represents the amount of requests to each CIDs. The second column represents the amount of replicas of each CIDs. The third column represents the amount of different CIDs provided by each provider node. Each column is independent, encoding different CIDs and providers.

Requested CIDs	Replicated CIDs	CIDs per Provider
482, 620	12, 610	869, 734
290, 485	5, 274	213, 837
254, 132	4, 663	202, 947
213, 019	2, 047	200, 373
209, 913	1, 876	176, 180
203, 510	1, 822	174, 803
199, 628	1, 404	173, 315
198, 500	1, 372	144, 422
193, 432	1, 283	108, 023
138, 084	1, 272	107, 885

This shows that content requested from Asia has a higher popularity (i.e., the same CIDs are requested more often) than in the remainder of regions. Figure 3b complements the ECDF with the distributions of frequency of requests (shown on the y-axis in logarithmic scale) over the number of CIDs (shown on the x-axis in logarithmic). However, this shows that all regions seem to present a similar Zipf distribution albeit, with different proportions, that is proportional to the request rate originating from that region.

4.2   Providers

In this section we analyze the results from the perspective of providers. With this, we aim to answer questions #3 and #4 of our analysis. *How are providers geo-distributed in the system?* and *How is provided content distributed across providers in the system?*

The first question is answered by the results presented in Table 4 which shows the number of providers per continent. Notice that North America (NA) has almost as many providers as Europe (EU) and Asia (AS) together. This shows, that North America composes the largest portion of the content providers on the IPFS system (which is corroborated by previous studies [2,14]). Furthermore, notice the last two columns in the table, that represent providers that only had a relay address (labeled as Rl), meaning they were behind a NAT without a public address; and providers whose location information was unknown (labeled as Un), meaning there was no entry on the MaxMind database for those providers public IP address. As the location of Rl nodes is also unknown, from this point on all Rl nodes are considered as belonging to the Un category.

To answer question #4: *How is provided content distributed across providers in the system?* we analyze both the amount of content replication in the system (Fig. 4) and the amount of (different) content provided by each individual provider node in the system (Fig. 5).

Table 4. Providers geo-distribution.

	AF	AS	EU	NA	OC	SA	AN	Rl	Un
Providers	40	4959	5789	10983	431	104	1	2473	689

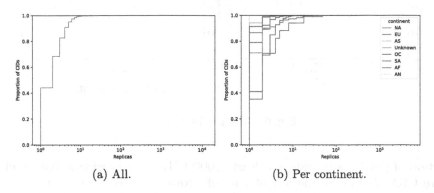

(a) All.   (b) Per continent.

Fig. 4. CID replicas.

Figure 4 reports on the amount of replicated content over different providers. Figure 4a shows an ECDF that captures the amount of replicas (on the x-axis in logarithmic scale) that were found for the proportion of CIDs in that were requested through the gateway (on the y-axis). We note that almost 70% of all CIDs are replicated at most twice (i.e., provided by at most two different providers in IPFS). Only a very small proportion of CIDs are replicated by a large number of providers. Table 3 summarizes the amount of replicas of the top 10 replicated CIDs, where, after looking into these CIDs, we found that most of them are IPFS manual pages. We verified if theses highly replicated CIDs were also the most requested CIDs and found that this was not the case. In fact, the top 10 requested CIDs are not highly replicated, having only a few providers (only 3 of these CIDs have more than 10 providers). Figure 4b breaks down the CID replicas by region. Here we notice that Africa has the most replicas of CIDs although, this does not represent a large number as there are only a few providers in that region. Although it is not visible in the plot, there is a small percentage of CIDs that is highly replicated in North America. This is not surprising, as North America has the largest number of content providers. Nevertheless, these results suggest that there is a very limited high availability of requested content through replication. This can be mostly explained by the way content is replicated, where there needs to be an explicit (re)provide action by the user after fetching a copy of the content from other provider(s).

Figure 5 shows the amount of different (requested) CIDs each provider provides. Figure 5a presents an ECDF of the proportion of providers (on the y-axis) that provide different amounts of CIDs (on the x-axis in logarithmic scale), here we can see that 60% of providers only provide a single CID. We also note that less than 10% of providers provide at least 10 CIDs, with a very small pro-

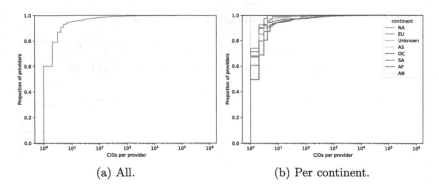

(a) All.   (b) Per continent.

Fig. 5. CIDs per provider.

portion of providers providing at least $1,000$ CIDs. The providers that provide more CIDs amount to the largest part of provided CIDs, meaning that most CIDs are provided by the same small set of providers. This suggests that pinning services are the main providers of content in IPFS. Table 3 summarizes the top 10 providers with the most CIDs. Some of these providers had DNS multi-address, which we verified pointed to DNS records suggesting these providers belonged to nft.storage, which is a popular storage service for NFT content in IPFS. Figure 5b analyzes the proportion of providers (on the y-axis) that provide different amounts of CIDs (on the x-axis in logarithmic scale) categorized by continent, which shows that the large providers are mostly located in North America (NA), Europe (EU), and Oceania (OC). The fact that the biggest portion of CIDs is provided only by a small set of providers suggests that although IPFS is a decentralized content network system, the content stored in IPFS presents a high degree of centralization in this small set of providers.

4.3 Requested Content Vs. Provided Content

Finally, in this section we combine gathered data from the requests and the providers to obtain a global view of the workload, and to answer the last question: *How does the location of requested content correlate with the location of providers for requested content?*

To this end, we matched the request's origin location to the providers' location, generating a heatmap (presented in Fig. 6) that matches the location from where each request was made to the location of provider(s) that had the requested content. In Fig. 6 the rows represent the location of the origin of (all) requests while the columns present the location of providers, including a column (and row) labelled as *Unknown* that encodes the percentage of requests to content whose provider was not found or did not have (valid) geolocation information. Note that a single request can be served by multiple locations, as per the CID replication factor we discussed previously. We normalized the requests per region to eliminate the disparity in quantity of requests, showing on the heatmap the percentage of all requests made from one region to any other region (including itself).

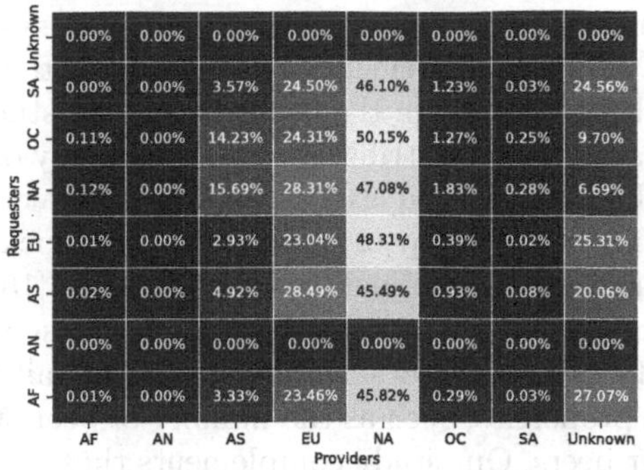

Requesters \ Providers	AF	AN	AS	EU	NA	OC	SA	Unknown
Unknown	0.00%	0.00%	0.00%	0.00%	0.00%	0.00%	0.00%	0.00%
SA	0.00%	0.00%	3.57%	24.50%	46.10%	1.23%	0.03%	24.56%
OC	0.11%	0.00%	14.23%	24.31%	50.15%	1.27%	0.25%	9.70%
NA	0.12%	0.00%	15.69%	28.31%	47.08%	1.83%	0.28%	6.69%
EU	0.01%	0.00%	2.93%	23.04%	48.31%	0.39%	0.02%	25.31%
AS	0.02%	0.00%	4.92%	28.49%	45.49%	0.93%	0.08%	20.06%
AN	0.00%	0.00%	0.00%	0.00%	0.00%	0.00%	0.00%	0.00%
AF	0.01%	0.00%	3.33%	23.46%	45.82%	0.29%	0.03%	27.07%

Fig. 6. Request locality of all requested content through the gateway.

By analyzing the heatmap, we notice that the vast majority of requests from all regions are either provided by providers in North America or in Europe. This in fact suggest that there is very little geographic locality access pattern in IPFS, as the heat is concentrated in North America and Europe, rather than on the diagonal of the heatmap. However, from our previous observations, this is also to be expected as the vast majority of content is located in these regions. Furthermore, from this heatmap we can conclude that the North American region contains the most popular CIDs, which from the previous observation that requests follow a Zipf distribution, we may also conclude that the Zipf is not independent per region. Finally, one last conclusion we can draw from our results is that the IPFS access patterns seems to be driven more by the content's popularity than by the local interests of users, and hence the locality assumption made by many P2P solutions is not applicable in this context. Indirectly, these findings also indicate that current dApps that really on IPFS for content distribution have a global expression, whose service providers are mostly located in North America and Europe.

5   Related Work

Measuring and understanding the behavior of large scale and decentralized systems has always been an important endeavour, with a vast amount of studies being made for peer-to-peer systems in the early 2000s. The main challenge in understanding how these systems operate in the wild derive from their decentralized nature, which makes it hard to have vantage points to collect enough information about events happening in the system. In particular, we highlight two studies over peer-to-peer systems, one that also analyzes the traffic of large scale systems, and a second that characterizes the workload of BitTorrent. The first [33] analyzes the peer-to-peer traffic across large networks such as Fast-Track, Gnutella, and DirectConnect, from the point of view of a single ISP. Their findings are similar to ours in the sense that they also observe most of the traffic being generated by a very small amount of hosts. The second study [29] analyzes the popular BitTorrent peer-to-peer file-sharing system. In this study, the authors perform active measurements in the systems to obtain data related to upload and download speeds. On the other hand, our study focuses on complementary aspects, such as the distribution and popularity of content published and accessed through IPFS and the access patterns to that content.

More recent studies on peer-to-peer systems include blockchain systems such as Bitcoin and Ethereum. Here we highlight two studies [15,19], that focus on the transactions made within Bitcoin and Ethereum blockchains. These studies characterize the performance of blockchain systems but fail to provide insights over system network properties, such as the number of peers per region or workload distribution over peers. Our study complements these by focusing on IPFS, an increasingly relevant building block in the Web3 ecosystem.

IPFS has been the subject of several recent studies [2,14] that are complementary to our own study, where the authors analyze peer distribution over geographical regions and Bitswap traffic inside IPFS. Furthermore, IPFS was extensively studied in [34], where the authors analyze the performance of the system in general. Our own study complements the previous findings through an analysis on the geographical relationship between IPFS web clients and content providers that previous studies did not accomplish, with the aim to characterize client access patterns to guide future research on IPFS and decentralized Web3 systems in general.

6   Conclusion

In this paper we presented a study over the traffic processed by one of the most popular public IPFS gateways to identify characteristics of the workload of a popular decentralized system and understand if IPFS would benefit from DHT designs that optimize a content sharing network assuming that there exists geographic locality on access patterns. In our study, we observed that the IPFS gateway mainly processes requests incoming from North America and Asia that target mostly the same content, independently of the location of the requester. To understand where was the content provided, we queried the network for the content provider records and discovered surprisingly that the most popular content fetched through the public IPFS gateway is provided by only a few nodes in the network. Our results suggest that IPFS is an imbalanced system centered on these few provider nodes, which would not benefit from a DHT design that access patterns follow geographic locality, as the access patterns seem to be driven by content popularity rather than geographic interest. On the other hand, this also points to studying novel load balancing schemes on IPFS that encourage IPFS (server) users to replicate popular content. As future work, we plan to extend our study to other public IPFS gateways as well as other Web3 networks, such as Ethereum Swarm and StorJ, to understand if our findings are generalizable to other decentralized Web3 systems. Furthermore, we plan to complement this study with a workload generator that produces client requests based on the observations of our study, to enable the research and practitioners community to evaluate Web3 (prototype) systems under realistic workloads.

References

1. Araujo, F., Rodrigues, L.: Geopeer: a location-aware peer-to-peer system. In: Proceedings of Third IEEE International Symposium on Network Computing and Applications (NCA 2004), pp. 39–46 (2004)
2. Balduf, L., Henningsen, S., Florian, M., Rust, S., Scheuermann, B.: Monitoring data requests in decentralized data storage systems: a case study of IPFS. In: 2022 IEEE 42nd ICDCS, IEEE (2022)
3. Benet, J.: IPFS - Content Addressed, Versioned, P2P File System. Technical Report Draft vol. 3 (2014)
4. Berty. Berty: the privacy-first messaging app. https://berty.tech/ (2022) Accessed Oct 2022
5. ConsenSys. Consensys: Ipfs look up measurement. https://github.com/ConsenSys/ipfs-lookup-measurement/ (2022). Accessed Feb 2022
6. Costa, P., Leitão, J., Psaras, Y.: Anonymised IPFS gateway logs from 7th of March of 2022 to 21st of March of 2022. https://doi.org/10.5281/zenodo.7876622, April 2023
7. D'Ambrosio, M., Dannewitz, C., Karl, H., Vercellone, V.: Mdht: a hierarchical name resolution service for information-centric networks. In: Proceedings of the ACM SIGCOMM Workshop on Information-Centric Networking, ICN 2011, pp. 7–12, New York, NY, USA, Association for Computing Machinery (2011)
8. de la Rocha, A., Dias, D., Yiannis, P.: A multi-path file transfer protocol in IPFs and filecoin. Technical report, Accelerating content routing with bitswap (2021)
9. Discussify. Discussify. https://github.com/ipfs-shipyard/pm-discussify (2022). Accessed Oct 2022
10. Fleek. Fleek: build on the new internet. https://fleek.co/, (2022). Accessed Oct 2022
11. BitTorrent Foundation. Bittorrent (btt) white paper. https://www.bittorrent.com/btt/btt-docs/BitTorrent_(BTT)_White_Paper_v0.8.7_Feb_2019.pdf (2019)
12. Grobauer, B., Walloschek, T., Stocker, E.: Understanding cloud computing vulnerabilities. IEEE Secur. Priv. 9(2), 50–57 (2011)
13. Gross, C., Stingl, D., Richerzhagen, B., Hemel, A., Steinmetz, R., Hausheer, D.: Geodemlia: a robust peer-to-peer overlay supporting location-based search. In: 2012 IEEE 12th International Conference on Peer-to-Peer Computing (P2P), pp. 25–36 (2012)
14. Henningsen, S., Florian, M., Rust, S., Scheuermann, B.: Mapping the interplanetary filesystem. In: 2020 IFIP Networking Conference (Networking) (2020)
15. Heo, H., Shin, S.: Behind block explorers: public blockchain measurement and security implication. In: 2021 IEEE 41st ICDCS (2021)
16. Korpal, G., Scott, D.: Decentralization and web3 technologies. Technical report, May 2022
17. Kovacevic, A., Liebau, N., Steinmetz, R.: Globase.kom - a p2p overlay for fully retrievable location-based search. In: 2007 7th International Conference on Peer-to-Peer Computing, pp. 87–96, Los Alamitos, CA, USA, IEEE Computer Society, September 2007
18. Kumar, S., Gautam, H., Singh, S., Shafeeq, M.: Top vulnerabilities in cloud computing. ECS Trans. 107(1), 16887 (2022)
19. Lee, X.T., Khan, A., Gupta, S.S., Ong, Y.H., Liu, X.: Measurements, analyses, and insights on the entire ethereum blockchain network. In: Proceedings of The Web Conference 2020, WWW '20 (2020)

20. Leitão, J.: Gossip-based broadcast protocols. Master's thesis, Faculdade de Ciências da Universidade de Lisboa (2007)
21. Leitao, J., Marques, J.P., Pereira, J.O., Rodrigues, L.: X-bot: a protocol for resilient optimization of unstructured overlays. In: 2009 28th IEEE International Symposium on Reliable Distributed Systems, pp. 236–245 (2009)
22. Leitão, J., Marques, J.P., Pereira, J.O., Rodrigues, L.: X-bot: a protocol for resilient optimization of unstructured overlay networks. IEEE Trans. Parallel Distrib. Syst. **23**(11), 2175–2188 (2012)
23. Leitão, J.: Topology management for unstructured overlay networks. Phd thesis (2010)
24. MaxMind. Maxmind - geolite2 free geolocation data. https://dev.maxmind.com/geoip/geolite2-free-geolocation-data?lang=en (2022). Accessed Oct 2022
25. Maymounkov, P., Mazières, D.: Kademlia: a peer-to-peer information system based on the XOR metric. In: Druschel, P., Kaashoek, F., Rowstron, A. (eds.) IPTPS 2002. LNCS, vol. 2429, pp. 53–65. Springer, Heidelberg (2002). https://doi.org/10.1007/3-540-45748-8_5
26. Monteiro, J., Costa, P.A., Leitão, J., de la Rocha, A., Psaras, Y.: Enriching kademlia by partitioning. In: Proceedings of the 1st Workshop on Decentralized Internet, Networks, Protocols, and Systems (DINPS'22) colocated with ICDCS (2022)
27. Nakamoto, S.: Bitcoin: a peer-to-peer electronic cash system. Decentralized Bus. Rev. (2008)
28. NFT.STORAGE. Nft storage: Free storage for NFTS. https://nft.storage/ (2022). Accessed Oct 2022
29. Pouwelse, J., Garbacki, P., Epema, D., Sips, H.: The Bittorrent P2P file-sharing system: measurements and analysis. In: Castro, M., van Renesse, R. (eds.) IPTPS 2005. LNCS, vol. 3640, pp. 205–216. Springer, Heidelberg (2005). https://doi.org/10.1007/11558989_19
30. Protocol Labs. libp2p: a modular network stack. https://libp2p.io (2022). Accessed Feb 2022
31. Ratti, S., Hariri, B., Shirmohammadi, S.: Nl-dht: a non-uniform locality sensitive DHT architecture for massively multi-user virtual environment applications. In: 2008 14th IEEE International Conference on Parallel and Distributed Systems, pp. 793–798 (2008)
32. Rodrigues, R., Druschel, P.: Peer-to-peer systems. Commun. ACM **53**(10), 72–82 (2010)
33. Sen, S., Wang, J.: Analyzing peer-to-peer traffic across large networks. In: Proceedings of the 2nd ACM SIGCOMM Workshop on Internet Measurment, IMW 2002 (2002)
34. Trautwein, D.: Design and evaluation of IPFs: a storage layer for the decentralized web. In: Proceedings of the ACM SIGCOMM 2022 Conference, SIGCOMM 2022 (2022)
35. Uniswap. Uniswap protocol: swap, earn, and build on the leading decentralized crypto trading protocol. https://uniswap.org/ (2022). Accessed Oct 2022
36. Wood, G.: Ethereum: a secure decentralised generalised transaction ledger. Technical report (2014)

Community-Based Gossip Algorithm for Distributed Averaging

Christel Sirocchi[1]([✉]) [iD] and Alessandro Bogliolo[1,2] [iD]

[1] DiSPeA, University of Urbino, Piazza della Repubblica 13, 61029 Urbino, PU, Italy
`c.sirocchi2@campus.uniurb.it`
[2] Digit srl, Corso Giuseppe Garibaldi 66, 61029 Urbino, PU, Italy

Abstract. Most real-world networks tend to organise according to an underlying modular structure, where nodes are relatively more connected with nodes belonging to the same community than others. Modularity can impact the performance of distributed data aggregation and computation in networked systems due to limited communication between communities. This paper examines the effects of modularity in the context of distributed averaging, a fundamental cooperative control problem and a central task in various applications ranging from clock synchronisation to formation control. Numerical experiments on synthetic networks demonstrate that modularity negatively affects the convergence rate of randomised gossip algorithms for distributed averaging. Further analysis suggests that nodes bridging communities (here termed boundary nodes) hold a crucial role in controlling the information flow across the network and that a modularity metric dependent on boundary nodes is a good linear predictor of performance while computable in a distributed manner. The averaging gossip protocol is then integrated with a distributed community detection algorithm, giving rise to a novel gossip scheme that leverages local community structure to improve performance by balancing the information flow at boundary nodes. The proposed community-based gossip algorithm is evaluated on synthetic modular structures, and its improved performance is confirmed by simulations run on real-world peer-to-peer networks. These findings emphasise the importance of community structure in distributed computation and might inspire further investigation in this direction.

Keywords: Distributed community detection · Distributed averaging · Gossip algorithms · Community structure · Peer-to-peer networks

1 Introduction

A fundamental property of almost every type of real-world network is the tendency to organise according to an underlying modular structure, referred to as community structure, where groups of nodes have relatively more connections among themselves than with the rest of the network. Modularity is likely to affect

© IFIP International Federation for Information Processing 2023
Published by Springer Nature Switzerland AG 2023
M. Patiño-Martínez and J. Paulo (Eds.): DAIS 2023, LNCS 13909, pp. 37–53, 2023.
https://doi.org/10.1007/978-3-031-35260-7_3

the performance of algorithms deployed on network systems, although such characterisations are still lacking in the literature. The sparse connections between communities (here termed *boundary edges*) are characteristic of modular structures and constitute communication bottlenecks for the network. The nodes at the ends of these links (referred to as *boundary nodes*) play a crucial role in the network, having privileged access to information from other communities and the duty of propagating it within their own. By providing nodes with knowledge of their local community structure, they become aware of their role within the network (boundary or *interior* node) and can act appropriately to improve the information flow. For instance, boundary nodes might reduce communication with neighbours of the same community, assuming that the propagated information is partly redundant, to favour exchanges with other communities.

This study leverages community structure to improve the performance of the *standard randomised gossip* algorithm for distributed averaging introduced by Boyd et al. [4], aimed at calculating the global average of a set of values by iterating local pair-wise computations. The experimental results demonstrate that the algorithm performance is influenced by the modular network structure and particularly by the proportion of boundary nodes. These nodes are also found to be statistically more central within the network and more accurate in their estimate of the global average. In light of these findings, a distributed community detection approach consistent with the averaging protocol and a gossip scheme leveraging community structure are introduced. Community detection informs nodes of their local community membership, as well as their role as boundary nodes bridging communities. The novel gossip scheme assigns boundary nodes an equal probability of interacting with each neighbouring community, thus balancing the information flow across the boundaries and improving performance.

The contributions of the work are as follows:

- to provide evidence that modularity affects the performance of the randomised distributed averaging algorithm;
- to offer a modularity metric predictive of performance and computable in a distributed manner;
- to propose a gossip scheme that boosts distributed averaging performance by taking into account the local community structure;

The remainder of the paper is organised as follows. Section 2 provides the relevant background on averaging gossip algorithms. Section 3 presents convergence results and topology-informed strategies from previous work, while Sect. 4 outlines the proposed community-based approach. Experimental methods are detailed in Sect. 5, and the results are presented and discussed in Sect. 6. Finally, conclusions and directions for future work are drawn in Sect. 7.

2   Background

Communication constraints in networked systems can be conveniently modelled by a graph $G = (V, E)$, where V is the vertex set of n nodes v_i, with $i \in$

$I = \{1,\ldots,n\}$ and $n \in N$, and E is the edge set $E \subseteq V \times V$ of the pairs $e_{ij} = (v_i, v_j)$, so that there is an edge between nodes v_i and v_j iff $(v_i, v_j) \in E$. The set of the nodes that can communicate with v_i (or neighbours) is denoted by $\Omega_i = \{v_j : (v_i, v_j) \in E\}$. The degree of v_i is then defined as $deg(v_i) = |\Omega_i|$, where $|.|$ is the cardinality of the set. The graph G is connected iff a path connecting v_i, and v_j exists $\forall\ i, j \in I$. G is termed simple if it is unweighted, undirected, without loops and multiple edges, meaning that the pairs $e_{ij} \in E$, with $i \neq j$, are unique, unordered, and are not assigned a weight.

2.1 Distributed Averaging

Let x_i denote the value of node v_i, representing a state, an opinion or a physical quantity such as position, temperature, or voltage, and $\mathbf{x} = (x_1, ..., x_n)^T$ the vector of values so that the ith component of $\mathbf{x}$ is the value at node v_i. The vector $\mathbf{x}(k)$ denotes the vector of values at time-slot k, while $\mathbf{x}(t)$ represents the continuous counterpart at time t. The system reaches asymptotic consensus if all nodes asymptotically converge to the same value, i.e. there exists x^* such that

$$\lim_{t \to +\infty} x_i(t) = x^*, \forall i \in I. \tag{1}$$

In distributed averaging, the goal is for x^* to be equal to the average of the initial values x_{avg}, computed as $\frac{1}{n} \sum_{i=1}^{n} x_i(0)$.

2.2 Gossip Algorithms

Gossip algorithms perform distributed averaging by realising asynchronous and randomised interaction schemes. The standard randomised gossip algorithm with *asynchronous time model* proposed by Boyd et al. [4] marks the passing of time with clocks assigned to each node and ticking at the times of a rate 1 Poisson process so that time can be discretised according to clock ticks. If the clock of node v_i ticks at time-slot k, the node randomly selects one of its neighbours v_j for interaction, and the two nodes perform local averaging:

$$x_i(k+1) = x_j(k+1) = \frac{x_i(k) + x_j(k)}{2}. \tag{2}$$

Each iteration is then characterised by the $n \times n$ matrix of the averaging weights $\mathbf{W} = [w_{ij}]$, so that the vector of values is updated as

$$\mathbf{x}(k+1) = \mathbf{W}(k)\mathbf{x}(k). \tag{3}$$

The interaction between v_i and v_j has weight matrix $\mathbf{W}_{ij}$ with elements equal to $\frac{1}{2}$ at $w_{ii}, w_{ij}, w_{jj}, w_{ji}$, equal to 1 at w_{kk}, with $k \neq i, j$, and 0 otherwise. The gossip scheme is defined by the $n \times n$ probability matrix $\mathbf{P} = [p_{ij}]$, prescribing the probability p_{ij} that the node v_i selects node v_j for interaction. In *random selection* [30], each node chooses any neighbour with equal probability, so

$$p_{ij} = \frac{1}{deg(v_i)} \ \forall v_j \in \Omega_i, \text{and 0 otherwise.}$$

3   Previous Work

This section presents the key convergence results for averaging gossip algorithms and reviews the main strategies developed over the past two decades to enhance their performance with respect to system requirements. This brief overview emphasises that the convergence rate of gossip algorithms is determined by the structural properties of the underlying communication network and highlights how alternative approaches leverage this knowledge to improve performance.

Distributed averaging is a central problem in distributed computation with wide-ranging applications, including coordinating and maintaining distributed power systems, synchronising clocks, live monitoring, and data fusion in sensor networks [20]. Averaging schemes can be adapted to compute other linear functions as well as more general calculations [3]. Averaging local information over a network is also a subroutine at the heart of many distributed optimisation algorithms, whose efficiency is crucial for the method's overall performance [12].

Gossip algorithms have become popular in distributed systems as simple and robust message-passing schemes for information processing over networks and have found application in distributed averaging with protocols such as Push-Pull Gossiping, Push-Sum, Distributed Random Grouping and Flow Updating [18]. However, a significant and well-known drawback of this approach is the slow convergence due to the transmission of redundant information. In complete graphs and certain types of well-connected structures (including expanders and small-world networks), the *standard randomised gossip* algorithm for distributed averaging is very efficient, requiring $\Theta(n\ log\ e^{-1})$ messages to converge to the global average within e accuracy [19]. In contrast, in grids and random geometric graphs, which are the relevant topologies for wireless sensor networks and many other distributed systems, even its optimised version converges very slowly, requiring $\Theta(n^2\ log\ e^{-1})$ transmissions, the same asymptotic quantity needed for every node to flood its estimate to all other nodes [8]. The seminal paper of Boyd et al. [4] provides a tight characterisation for the convergence time of standard gossip in any connected graph dependent on the second largest eigenvalue of the averaging weights expected matrix, which is entirely specified by the network topology and the node selection probabilities. Their work further addresses the problem of optimising the neighbour selection probabilities to accelerate convergence in centralised and distributed settings.

Several efforts have been devoted to reducing the transmissions required by averaging gossip algorithms to enhance performance, mitigate resource consumption, and prolong system lifetime. Some of the approaches leverage either the properties of the network or the communication medium to improve convergence. The *geographic gossip* algorithm utilises greedy geographic routing to construct an overlay network that enables multi-hop communication between any pair of nodes [7]. The algorithm reduces the complexity by $\sqrt{n\ /\ log\ n}$ over the standard gossip algorithm but assumes that nodes are aware of their own and their neighbours' geographic locations. The *geographic gossip with path averaging* extends this protocol by averaging nodes along the routed paths and requiring only $\Theta(n\ log\ e^{-1})$ messages, with each message packet needing to be routed back on the same path to disseminate the computed average [3]. A lightweight algorithm based on simple virtual coordinates extends the geographic approach to networks whose nodes are unaware of their geographic location [14].

Broadcasting-based gossiping leverages the inherently broadcast nature of the wireless medium and achieves the fastest rate of convergence among all gossip algorithms without the need for complex routing or pair-wise exchange operations but requires out-degree information for each node to converge to the global average [2]. In *broadcast gossip*, nodes within the predefined radius of the broadcasting node receive the value and perform an update. Modifications to this algorithm guarantee convergence to the average while removing previous assumptions [33]. The *greedy gossip with eavesdropping* selects for interaction the two nodes having the maximum difference between values based on broadcasted data [32]. In contrast, the *neighbourhood gossip* algorithm exploits local interference in wireless medium to perform computations over a larger local neighbourhood and reduces the communication complexity of the baseline gossip algorithm by a factor of q^2, where q is the neighbourhood size [25].

Further strategies consider power consumption in performance evaluation and design of efficient algorithms. Selecting nodes for interaction according to the power of two choices scheme enables balancing the energy levels of gossiping nodes, leading to more uniform energy expenditure across the network [13]. Alternatively, the joint optimisation of the total power consumption and the second largest eigenvalue of the expected weight matrix realises a trade-off between the communication burden and convergence rate [35].

Geometric random graphs are the baseline topology for most approaches, although alternative structures are also being investigated. A distributed averaging gossip algorithm developed specifically for ring networks ensures convergence within a finite number of communication rounds [11]. The convergence analysis of a one-dimensional lattice network provides novel insights into the influence of gossip weight and network structure on performance [21]. In *periodic gossiping* [16], where pairs of nodes interact periodically in a predetermined schedule, the convergence rate exhibits unusual characteristics in tree topologies [34].

Recent studies have been focusing on distributed averaging as a central subroutine in large-scale optimisation problems, particularly in the realm of machine learning [31]. In distributed deep learning, training a model on a massive dataset can be expedited by partitioning the data across multiple machines and performing mini-batch gradient updates. In these distributed systems, nodes must communicate to coordinate their computation and synchronise their variables, often using distributed averaging [1]. Recent research has investigated how the network topology influences the performance of distributed solvers and their distributed averaging subroutines [12, 26].

The impact of topology on the convergence rate of averaging gossip algorithms is well-established, and topology-guided approaches have been shown to be effective. However, the effect of community structure has not been thoroughly investigated, let alone utilised to improve performance. The objective of this study is to address this research gap.

4   Community-Based Gossip Protocol

Gossip with random selection guarantees that a node communicates uniformly with all its neighbours but does not consider the quality of the exchanged information. In modular structures, the uneven edge density causes redundant message passing within groups and inefficient information propagation between communities. Boundary nodes, shown in Fig. 1(b) for the network in Fig. 1(a), are crucial in mediating these sparse transmissions. Still, under random selection, they interact more with nodes of their own community than the others. The proposed gossip scheme, *community selection*, mitigates this limitation by assigning an equal interaction probability to communities rather than nodes.

To this end, the standard gossip protocol for distributed averaging presented in Sect. 2.2 is coupled with a *Label Propagation Algorithm* (LPA) for distributed community detection to map boundary nodes and deploy more efficient gossip schemes with minimal memory and communication overhead per node. The study adopts an asynchronous LPA with Prec-Max tie-breaking strategy [5]. Although the asynchronous LPA is less efficient than the synchronous counterpart, it guarantees convergence to stable labelling and does not require time to be commonly slotted across all nodes. The algorithm requires that each node is initially assigned a unique label and updates it at each iteration by choosing the most frequent label among its neighbours. If multiple choices are possible, the Prec-Max algorithm dictates that precedence is first given to the current label (Prec) and then to that with the highest value (Max).

The distributed averaging gossip algorithm can incorporate LPA, provided that nodes are assigned unique identifiers. This integrated gossip scheme, termed *LPA community selection*, requires that each node v_i stores its value x_i, its label l_i, and information of its neighbours labels l_j^i $\forall v_j \in \Omega_i$ over time. A partition $C^i = \{C_1^i, C_2^i, .., C_m^i\}$ of the neighbourhood Ω_i can be defined for v_i so that any two nodes v_j and v_k in Ω_i belong to the same community $C_n^i \in C^i$ iff $l_j^i = l_k^i$. Each node v_i initialise its label $l_i(0)$ with a unique identifier (e.g. its index i) and each neighbour's label with the identifier of the corresponding node, i.e. $l_j^i(0) = l_j(0)$ $\forall v_j \in \Omega_i$. In each gossip iteration at time-slot k, node v_i chooses a neighbour v_j to perform local averaging by dividing the interaction probability equally among the communities detected in its neighbourhood and then again equally among nodes of the same community. Formally:

$$p_{ij}(k) = \frac{1}{|\{C^i(k)\}| \cdot |\{v_h : v_h \in \Omega_i \wedge l_h^i(k) = l_j^i(k)\}|} \quad \forall v_j \in \Omega_i, \text{and 0 otherwise.}$$

(4)

The interaction between nodes v_i and v_j entails sharing their current estimates of the global average $x_i(k)$ and $x_j(k)$, as well as their current labels $l_i(k)$ and $l_j(k)$. Then, the nodes update their estimate according to Eq. 2 and their knowledge of the neighbour's label, so that $l_j^i(k+1) = l_j(k)$ and $l_i^j(k+1) = l_i(k)$. Finally, the nodes update their own label according to the Prec-Max criterion defined above. Figure 1(d) exemplifies label propagation for the network in Fig. 1(a), converging to the stable labelling shown in Fig. 1(c).

The proposed method performs community mapping and distributed averaging simultaneously, updating interaction probabilities as labels change until stable labelling is attained, thus enabling the mapping of dynamic communities. Nevertheless, the two tasks need not be coupled. Community structure may be available as ground truth or mapped ahead using methods other than LPA that, for instance, do not require unique node identifiers. In such cases, each node v_i is assigned a constant label L_i identifying its community membership and a stable partition $\mathcal{C} = \{C_1, C_2, .., C_k\}$ of the node set V can be defined so that any two nodes v_i and v_j in V belong to the same community $C_n \in \mathcal{C}$ iff $L_i = L_j$. Given this context, the proposed gossip scheme, termed *known community selection*, utilises the standard randomised gossip algorithm with interaction probability according to the community selection criterion, which is time-invariant and defined as:

$$p_{ij} = \frac{1}{|\{C_n : C_n \cap \Omega_i \neq 0\}| \cdot |\{v_h : v_h \in \Omega_i \wedge L_h = L_j\}|} \quad \forall v_j \in \Omega_i \text{ and } 0 \text{ otherwise.}$$
(5)

Notably, LPA community selection reduces to known community selection once the network has reached stable labelling and each node has communicated its label to all its neighbours. The proposed approach balances the information exchanged at boundary nodes while it is equivalent to the random selection for interior nodes. In the absence of a modular structure, as in Erdős-Rényi graphs, rings or lattices, community detection yields a partition with a single set, reducing community selection to random selection.

5 Experimental Methodology

The methods are articulated as follows: Sect. 5.1 presents the metrics chosen to quantify the graph structural properties and the algorithm performance; Sect. 5.2 describes the synthetic and real-world networks investigated; Sect. 5.3 overviews the software deployed to run gossip algorithms on networks.

5.1 Metrics

The study considers degree, clustering, modularity, and community metrics to investigate the relationship between structural features and the algorithm performance, as well as to guarantee that the generated network set is sufficiently varied and representative of real-world scenarios.

Degree metrics quantify the degree distribution and degree mixing pattern. These are the average degree (deg_{avg}), the standard deviation of the degree (deg_{std}), and the degree assortativity ($assort$), calculated as the Pearson correlation coefficient of the degrees of connected nodes.

Clustering metrics measure the tendency of connecting nodes to have shared neighbours. The clustering coefficient of a node is the number of existing triangles passing through that node divided by the number of all possible triangles. The average ($clust_{avg}$) and standard deviation ($clust_{std}$) are calculated for

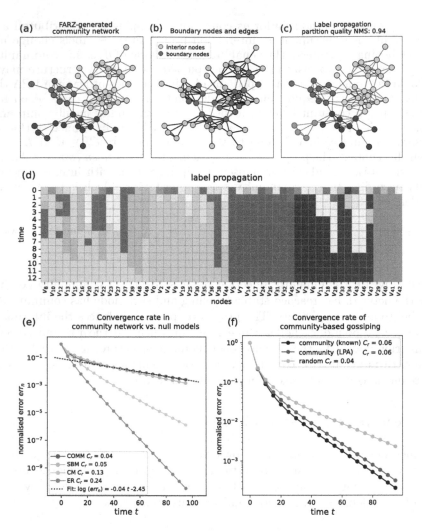

Fig. 1. (a) Community structure (COMM) generated using the FARZ benchmark [10] with parameters $n = 50, m = 4, h = 4, \beta = 0.9, \alpha = 0.5, \gamma = 0.5$ having medium-high modularity $mod = 0.62$. (b) Boundary and interior nodes (according to FARZ partition) and boundary edges shown as red lines. (c) The network partition returned by LPA, highlighting mismatches with FARZ ground truth. (d). The output of the asynchronous Prec-Max Label Propagation Algorithm (LPA) deployed on the same network. Node labels, remapped to a colour map to facilitate visualisation, are sampled at regular time points and reach stable labelling by $t = 11$. (e) Normalised error over time computed for the distributed averaging gossip algorithm with random selection simulated on COMM and its three null models Erdős-Rényi (ER), Configuration Model (CM), and Stochastic Block Model (SBM), averaged over 100 runs. The logarithm of the error decreases linearly with time, so the adopted performance metric, the convergence rate C_r, is the angular coefficient of this linear trend. (f) Convergence rate of gossip algorithms with random selection, community selection with known community structure, and community selection mapped by LPA run on the same network (error averaged over 100 runs). Averaging over a known structure yields a lower error than mapping communities with LPA, although the convergence rate is unchanged.

the clustering coefficients at nodes. Transitivity (*trans*) is defined similarly but at the network level as the fraction of all possible triangles that exist.

Community metrics record statistics calculated on community features, including the number of communities ($comm_n$) as well as the average ($comm_{avg}$) and standard deviation ($comm_{std}$) of their size.

Modularity metrics estimate the strength of the division of networks into modules. Modularity (*mod*) is defined as the fraction of the edges within a group minus the expected fraction of edges if these were distributed at random [27]. The study adopts two additional metrics that are simple, intuitive and, unlike modularity, computable in a distributed manner. The fraction of boundary edges (*fbe*) is the number of edges linking nodes of different communities over the total number of edges. The fraction of boundary nodes (*fbn*) is the number of nodes connected to nodes of other communities over the network size.

Performance metrics evaluate the convergence rate of the gossip algorithm independently of the distribution of the initial values. An established measure of convergence is the normalised error (err_n), defined as the norm of the error vector at time t divided by the norm of the initial state vector [4]:

$$err_n(t) = \frac{\|\mathbf{err}(t)\|}{\|\mathbf{x}(0)\|} = \frac{\|\mathbf{x}(t) - x_{avg}\mathbf{1}\|}{\|\mathbf{x}(0)\|},$$

where $\|.\|$ is the l_2 norm of the vector and $\mathbf{1}$ is the $n \times 1$ vector of all 1s. After a transient faster phase, the logarithm of err_n decreases linearly with time, so the convergence rate C_r can be defined as the angular coefficient of this linear stationary regime which, unlike err_n, is independent of time [6]:

$$log(err_n(t)) = -C_r\, t.$$

5.2   Networks

Synthetic Modular Networks. The study investigates a wide range of synthetic networks generated using the FARZ benchmark, which produces intrinsically modular networks for community evaluation and validation [10]. This model addresses three fundamental properties of complex networks, which other established benchmarks [15,22] cannot fully reproduce: heavy-tail degree distribution, high clustering, and community structure [36]. FARZ incorporates many tuning parameters to generate a wide range of experimental settings, enabling a thorough investigation of community structures [28]. The study generates and analyses a set of 1000 connected simple graphs of size $n = 1000$, referred to as the synthetic set. The network space is explored by sampling the following parameters in the corresponding interval: the number of communities h in [3, 25] (corresponding to the metric $comm_n$); the probability of forming edges within communities β in [0.5, 0.99] (quantifying the strength of communities); the number of edges created per node m in [2, 20] (controlling the average degree); the degree similarity coefficient α in [0.1, 0.9] (affecting the degree assortativity); and the common neighbour coefficient γ in [0.1, 0.9] (affecting transitivity). The FARZ model is designed to generate skewed node degree and community size distributions, as found in real networks. Graphs are required to be connected to guarantee convergence to the global average [4]. An example of a FARZ-generated network is shown in Fig. 1(a) with the respective parameters and community membership.

Null Models. The effect of modularity on performance is evaluated using three null models of increasing complexity: the Erdős-Rényi (ER) Model [9] preserves the number of nodes and edges, hence the network density; the Configuration Model (CM) [27] replicates the degree distribution but destroys degree-degree correlations; the Stochastic Block Model (SBM) [17] maintains the modular structure of the network, intended as the probability of nodes in any two communities to be connected. Null models are generated for three sets of 100 synthetic networks having the same size (n=1000), density (deg_{avg}=13), and community number (h=15) but increasing modularity (0.0, 0.5, 0.9), obtained by tuning the β parameter in the FARZ model. The comparison of convergences rates in a community network and the respective null models is exemplified in Fig. 1(e).

Real-World Networks. The study evaluates its findings on a peer-to-peer file-sharing systems. These networks are expected to display a degree of modularity as users are connected based on the available content. Moreover, such systems can benefit from optimising distributed averaging as they are primarily concerned with measuring global properties, such as the average size of shared files. The study analyses 9 snapshots of the Gnutella peer-to-peer file-sharing network taken on 9 different days in August 2002 [29] and made available by the Stanford Large Network Dataset Collection [23]. The networks have, on average, 21000 nodes and 56000 edges, representing Gnutella hosts and their connections.

5.3 Simulator

The study evaluates the standard randomised gossip algorithm with random selection described in Sect. 2.2, hereafter referred to as *random selection*, and the LPA community selection algorithm presented in Sect. 4, simply termed *community selection*. Known community selection was not included due to the requirement of community ground truth, which is not always available. Performance comparison of the averaging algorithms is exemplified in Fig. 1(f). The algorithm convergence rate is measured through event-driven simulations using a Python-based tool developed to characterise topological effects on performance [30]. The simulator requires three inputs: a graph for communication topology, a vector of initial node values, and a gossip criterion. The original tool was adapted to integrate community detection and was preferred over more established simulators for peer-to-peer networks, such as PeerSim [24], as it offers direct integration with the FARZ library for network generation and the NetworkX library for metrics calculations. The simulator, as well as the networks and data generated within the study, are available in the GitHub repository[1].

---

[1] https://github.com/ChristelSirocchi/gossip_modularity.

6   Results and Discussion

6.1   Effect of Modularity on Distributed Averaging Performance

The effect of community structure on performance in modular networks (COMM) is investigated by comparing the convergence rate of randomised gossip with that in the corresponding ER, CM and SBM null models, which preserve edge density, degree distribution and block structure, respectively (Table 1). The first simulation set runs the random gossip algorithm on 300 synthetic modular graphs and their respective null models, generated following the procedures outlined in Sect. 5.2. The convergence rate is measured for each network and averaged over 100 runs. Figure 2(a) shows that in the absence of any modular configuration (mod $\approx$ 0.0), the performance in SBM is not significantly different than that in ER because nodes are equally likely to interact with any community, so SBM reduces to ER. The convergence rate in SBM and ER, characterised by binomial degree distributions, is several times higher than that in CM, confirming that the degree distribution affects performance and that convergence is faster in statistically homogeneous networks. The performance in CM is closest to COMM's, although still significantly higher, suggesting that degree distribution is one but not the only factor affecting convergence. Clustering and degree assortativity, which CM does not replicate, are likely to introduce structural constraints and reduce performance. In weak community networks (mod $\approx$ 0.5), COMM's convergence is not significantly slower than in the previous case, suggesting that the degree distribution remains the primary determinant of performance. In contrast, for strong modular structures (mod $\approx$ 0.9), convergence is several times lower and indistinguishable from SBM's, suggesting that modularity determines performance in highly-modular networks.

Table 1. Metrics computed for a community network of size $n = 1000$ (COMM) and its Erdős-Rényi (ER), Configuration Model (CM), and Stochastic Block Model (SBM).

network	deg_{avg}	deg_{std}	$assort$	$trans$	$clust_{avg}$	$clust_{std}$	mod	$comm_{avg}$	$comm_{std}$	$comm_k$
COMM	12.91	10.32	0.37	0.53	0.48	0.26	0.87	71.43	17.02	15
SBM	12.88	3.45	0.10	0.15	0.15	0.06	0.87	71.43	17.02	15
CM	12.91	10.32	−0.01	0.03	0.03	0.07	–	–	–	–
ER	12.91	3.66	−0.01	0.01	0.01	0.02	–	–	–	–

6.2   Predictive Value of Modularity Metrics

The predictive power of structural metrics gauging degree distribution, clustering, and community structure is evaluated on the generated synthetic set. Simulations measure the convergence rate of the random gossip algorithm (averaged over 100 runs) and calculate the structural metrics detailed in Sect. 5.1 for each

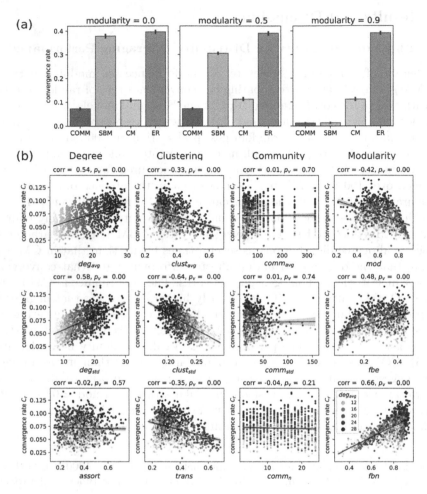

Fig. 2. (a) Convergence rate of the gossip averaging algorithm with random selection calculated for graphs all having $n = 1000$, $deg_{avg} = 13$ and $h = 15$, but different modularity mod (0.0, 0.5, 0.9), corresponding to absent, medium and robust community structure. Convergence rates are calculated for 300 community graphs (termed COMM), 100 graphs per modularity level, and the corresponding Erdős-Rényi (ER) models, Configuration Models (CM), and Stochastic Block Models (SBM), averaged over 100 runs. The error bar indicates the 95% confidence interval. **(b)** Scatter plot of 12 structural graph metrics vs. the convergence rate of the gossip algorithm with random selection, simulated on the FARZ-generated synthetic set of 1000 networks of size $n = 1000$ (convergence rate averaged over 100 runs). The considered metrics measure degree distribution, clustering, modularity and community size distribution of the networks. For each metric, the best-fit linear regression line is shown as a solid black line with 95% confidence interval, and the Pearson correlation coefficient ($corr$) and p-value (p_v) are provided above each plot. Plotted points are coloured according to the average degree of the corresponding graph to highlight any dependence of the selected metric on the degree, as in deg_{std} and $clust_{std}$.

network in the synthetic set, generated as described in Sect. 5.2. The results shown in Fig. 2(b) confirm the expected positive correlation between average degree and performance, as denser graphs propagate messages faster, and the negative effect of clustering, which promotes the diffusion of redundant information. Community number and size have no predictive power over the algorithm performance, while all modularity measures record a medium-high Pearson's correlation coefficient ($-0.42, 0.48, 0.66$ for mod, fbe and fbn, respectively). In networks of a given size and density, fbn holds the highest explanatory value (r-squared $= 0.55$), followed by fbe (r-squared $= 0.50$) and mod (r-squared $= 0.42$). These findings suggest that the simple and intuitive modularity measure based on the boundary nodes proposed in this study, fbn, is a superior linear predictor of performance than the standard modularity metric and confirm the crucial role of boundary nodes in information propagation within modular networks. Furthermore, this global metric can be computed distributively by the network and adopted by each node to evaluate the algorithm performance in light of modularity. Nodes can use their knowledge of local community membership to determine their role in the network, setting a label to 1 if they are boundary nodes and 0 otherwise. Estimating the fraction of boundary nodes can then be achieved by distributed averaging over the labels, possibly in conjunction with the measured quantity, with minimal overhead for the system.

6.3   Structural and Functional Properties of Boundary Nodes

The critical structural role of boundary nodes given by their privileged position in the graph is confirmed by evaluating their centrality and the accuracy of the estimated average. The proposed LPA community selection algorithm is run on each network in the synthetic set to map boundary and interior nodes. Four centrality metrics (degree, betweenness, closeness, and eigenvalue) are calculated for all nodes and centrality averages are computed for the two node sets (boundary and interior nodes). To evaluate the accuracy of nodes estimates, the normalised error err_n is calculated for the two node sets at time intervals of 5 up to t=100, and the error over the entire interval is calculated as the l_2-norm of the error vector. Figure 3(a) shows that centrality is significantly higher in boundary nodes for all metrics and many folds greater for betweenness centrality, which is often adopted to identify bridging positions and communications bottlenecks. It should be noted that centrality metrics are computationally expensive, requiring up to $O(n^3)$ computations in dense graphs and complete knowledge of the network structure. Therefore, distributed community detection enables identifying central nodes in community structures without costly calculations and in a distributed manner. In the considered distributed averaging scenario, privileged access to novel information is reflected in more accurate predictions of the global average. The normalised error calculated at time points and over a time interval is significantly lower at boundary nodes than at interior nodes, as shown in Fig. 3(b) and (c). Paired T-test confirms these differences to be significant (p-value = e-65). It follows that tasks that require elaborating and communicating the global average should be performed by boundary nodes, as they hold

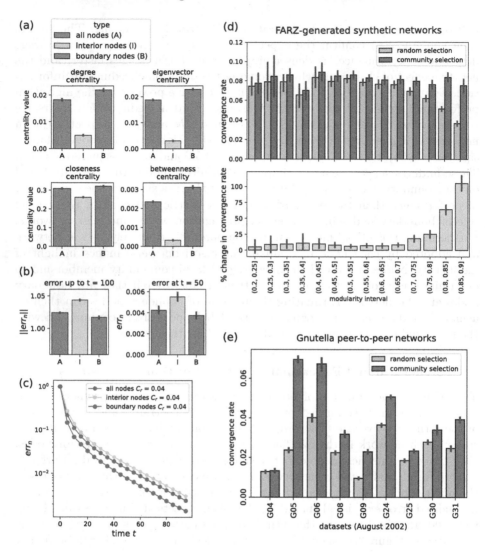

Fig. 3. (a) Average degree, eigenvector, closeness and betweenness centrality calculated on all nodes, boundary nodes and interior nodes in 1000 synthetic community networks. Boundary nodes record higher values for all four centrality metrics. (b) Normalised error calculated over the time interval [0,100] and normalised error at the intermediate time t = 50 calculated on all nodes, boundary nodes and interior nodes in the same synthetic set. Both error measurements are significantly lower for boundary nodes. (c) Normalised error over time calculated at boundary, interior and all nodes for the network in Fig. 1(a). Error is lower at boundary nodes, although the convergence rate is equal in the two subsets. (d) Convergence rates of gossip algorithms with random and community selection, simulated on the synthetic set and stratified based on modularity. The percentage performance increase for community selection increases with modularity. (e) Convergence rates of gossip algorithms with random and community selection simulated on 9 snapshots of the Gnutella peer-to-peer file-sharing system.

more accurate estimates. Therefore, community detection provides homogeneous networked systems with a tool to identify the most critical nodes without any centralised control or knowledge of the global structure.

6.4 Performance of Community-Based Gossip

The LPA-generated partition is evaluated on the synthetic set against the FARZ ground truth communities using the Normalised Mutual Information (NMI) score. Highly modular networks ($mod > 0.9$) report NMI scores consistently higher than 0.95, while weaker community structures ($0.5 > mod > 0.9$) have NMI above 0.7, confirming the efficacy of the LPA mapping method. The most frequent labelling discrepancies concern individual nodes bordering communities and large clusters being broken into smaller ones, as seen in Fig. 1(c) for the network in Fig. 1(a). The proposed approach is evaluated on the synthetic set by measuring the convergence rates of random selection and LPA community selection (averaged over 100 runs). In structures with modularity below 0.7, convergence is, on average, 10% higher than random selection, although these differences are not statistically significant. However, as modularity increases from 0.7 to 0.9, the performance of random selection drops, while that of community selection is stable and significantly higher than the random counterpart (20% higher at $mod = 0.7$, 100% at $mod = 0.9$), as shown in Fig. 3(d). The gossip algorithms are then compared on real-world peer-to-peer networks sampled from the Gnutella file-sharing system, characterised by $n \approx 10^5$ nodes and medium-low modularity (≈ 0.4), averaging convergence rates over 20 runs due to their large size. Community selection is significantly faster in 8 out 9 datasets, as shown in Fig. 3(e), and up to 3 times faster as in dataset "G05".

7   Conclusions

This study shed light on the effect of community structure and the critical role of boundary nodes in the performance of asynchronous distributed averaging algorithms in modular networks. The proposed approach deploys community detection by label propagation to identify boundary nodes in a distributed manner and proposes a novel gossip scheme that leverages local community structure to balance the information flow across community boundaries. Numerical experiments in synthetic and real-world modular systems confirm the faster convergence of this algorithm. This study contributes to the growing body of research on leveraging topological information to improve algorithm performance, and its findings have practical implications for the design of distributed algorithms in community networks. Future efforts will be devoted to providing a formal and empirical characterisation of the proposed gossip scheme with mapped and known community structure, and investigating more realistic scenarios (e.g. time delays, switching topologies) leveraging existing peer-to-peer simulators.

References

1. Assran, M., Loizou, N., Ballas, N., Rabbat, M.: Stochastic gradient push for distributed deep learning. In: International Conference on Machine Learning, pp. 344–353. PMLR (2019)
2. Aysal, T.C., Yildiz, M.E., Sarwate, A.D., Scaglione, A.: Broadcast gossip algorithms for consensus. IEEE Trans. Signal Process. **57**(7), 2748–2761 (2009)
3. Bénézit, F., Dimakis, A.G., Thiran, P., Vetterli, M.: Order-optimal consensus through randomized path averaging. IEEE Trans. Inf. Theory **56**(10), 5150–5167 (2010)
4. Boyd, S., Ghosh, A., Prabhakar, B., Shah, D.: Randomized gossip algorithms. IEEE Trans. Inf. Theory **52**(6), 2508–2530 (2006)
5. Cordasco, G., Gargano, L.: Community detection via semi-synchronous label propagation algorithms. In: 2010 IEEE International Workshop on: Business Applications of Social Network Analysis (BASNA), pp. 1–8. IEEE (2010)
6. Denantes, P., Bénézit, F., Thiran, P., Vetterli, M.: Which distributed averaging algorithm should i choose for my sensor network? In: IEEE INFOCOM 2008-The 27th Conference on Computer Communications, pp. 986–994. IEEE (2008)
7. Dimakis, A.D., Sarwate, A.D., Wainwright, M.J.: Geographic gossip: efficient averaging for sensor networks. IEEE Trans. Signal Process. **56**(3), 1205–1216 (2008)
8. Dimakis, A.G., Kar, S., Moura, J.M., Rabbat, M.G., Scaglione, A.: Gossip algorithms for distributed signal processing. Proc. IEEE **98**(11), 1847–1864 (2010)
9. Erdős, P., Rényi, A., et al.: On the evolution of random graphs. Publ. Math. Inst. Hung. Acad. Sci **5**(1), 17–60 (1960)
10. Fagnan, J., Abnar, A., Rabbany, R., Zaiane, O.R.: Modular networks for validating community detection algorithms. arXiv preprint arXiv:1801.01229 (2018)
11. Falsone, A., Margellos, K., Garatti, S., Prandini, M.: Finite-time distributed averaging over gossip-constrained ring networks. IEEE Trans. Control Netw. Syst. **5**(3), 879–887 (2017)
12. França, G., Bento, J.: Distributed optimization, averaging via ADMM, and network topology. Proc. IEEE **108**(11), 1939–1952 (2020)
13. Freschi, V., Lattanzi, E., Bogliolo, A.: Randomized gossip with power of two choices for energy aware distributed averaging. IEEE Commun. Lett. **19**(8), 1410–1413 (2015)
14. Freschi, V., Lattanzi, E., Bogliolo, A.: Accelerating distributed averaging in sensor networks: Randomized gossip over virtual coordinates. In: 2016 IEEE Sensors Applications Symposium (SAS), pp. 1–6. IEEE (2016)
15. Girvan, M., Newman, M.E.: Community structure in social and biological networks. Proc. Natl. Acad. Sci. **99**(12), 7821–7826 (2002)
16. He, F., Mou, S., Liu, J., Morse, A.S.: Convergence rate on periodic gossiping. Inf. Sci. **364**, 111–125 (2016)
17. Holland, P.W., Laskey, K.B., Leinhardt, S.: Stochastic blockmodels: first steps. Soc. Netw. **5**(2), 109–137 (1983)
18. Jesus, P., Baquero, C., Almeida, P.S.: A survey of distributed data aggregation algorithms. IEEE Commun. Surv. Tutor. **17**(1), 381–404 (2014)
19. Kempe, D., Dobra, A., Gehrke, J.: Gossip-based computation of aggregate information. In: Proceedings of 44th Annual IEEE Symposium on Foundations of Computer Science, pp. 482–491. IEEE (2003)
20. Khosravi, A., Kavian, Y.S.: Broadcast gossip ratio consensus: asynchronous distributed averaging in strongly connected networks. IEEE Trans. Signal Process. **65**(1), 119–129 (2016)

21. Kouachi, S., Dhuli, S., Singh, Y.N.: Convergence rate analysis of periodic gossip algorithms for one-dimensional lattice WSNs. IEEE Sens. J. **20**(21), 13150–13160 (2020)
22. Lancichinetti, A., Fortunato, S.: Community detection algorithms: a comparative analysis. Phys. Rev. E **80**(5), 056117 (2009)
23. Leskovec, J., Krevl, A.: SNAP Datasets: Stanford large network dataset collection (2014). https://snap.stanford.edu/data
24. Montresor, A., Jelasity, M.: PeerSim: a scalable P2P simulator. In: Proceedings of the 9th International Conference on Peer-to-Peer (P2P 2009), Seattle, WA, pp. 99–100 (2009)
25. Nazer, B., Dimakis, A.G., Gastpar, M.: Neighborhood gossip: concurrent averaging through local interference. In: 2009 IEEE International Conference on Acoustics, Speech and Signal Processing, pp. 3657–3660. IEEE (2009)
26. Nedić, A., Olshevsky, A., Rabbat, M.G.: Network topology and communication-computation tradeoffs in decentralized optimization. Proc. IEEE **106**(5), 953–976 (2018)
27. Newman, M.E.: The structure and function of complex networks. SIAM Rev. **45**(2), 167–256 (2003)
28. Pérez-Ortiz, M., Manescu, P., Caccioli, F., Fernández-Reyes, D., Nachev, P., Shawe-Taylor, J.: Network topological determinants of pathogen spread. Sci. Rep. **12**(1), 1–13 (2022)
29. Ripeanu, M., Foster, I.: Mapping the Gnutella network: macroscopic properties of large-scale peer-to-peer systems. In: Druschel, P., Kaashoek, F., Rowstron, A. (eds.) IPTPS 2002. LNCS, vol. 2429, pp. 85–93. Springer, Heidelberg (2002). https://doi.org/10.1007/3-540-45748-8_8
30. Sirocchi, C., Bogliolo, A.: Topological network features determine convergence rate of distributed average algorithms. Sci. Rep. **12**(1), 21831 (2022)
31. Tsianos, K.I., Rabbat, M.G.: Efficient distributed online prediction and stochastic optimization with approximate distributed averaging. IEEE Trans. Signal Inf. Process. Netw. **2**(4), 489–506 (2016)
32. Ustebay, D., Oreshkin, B.N., Coates, M.J., Rabbat, M.G.: Greedy gossip with eavesdropping. IEEE Trans. Signal Process. **58**(7), 3765–3776 (2010)
33. Wu, S., Liu, B., Bai, X., Hou, Y.: Eavesdropping-based gossip algorithms for distributed consensus in wireless sensor networks. IEEE Signal Process. Lett. **22**(9), 1388–1391 (2015)
34. Yu, C., Anderson, B.D., Mou, S., Liu, J., He, F., Morse, A.S.: Distributed averaging using periodic gossiping. IEEE Trans. Autom. Control **62**(8), 4282–4289 (2017)
35. Zhang, J.: Power optimized and power constrained randomized gossip approaches for wireless sensor networks. IEEE Wirel. Commun. Lett. **10**(2), 241–245 (2020)
36. Zuev, K., Boguná, M., Bianconi, G., Krioukov, D.: Emergence of soft communities from geometric preferential attachment. Sci. Rep. **5**(1), 1–9 (2015)

Data Management

Transactional Causal Consistent Microservices Simulator

Pedro Pereira and António Rito Silva(⊠)

INESC-ID, Instituto Superior Técnico, University of Lisbon, Lisbon, Portugal
{pedro.l.pereira,rito.silva}@tecnico.ulisboa.pt

Abstract. Microservice architecture has been widely adopted to develop software systems, but some of its trade-offs are often ignored. In particular, the introduction of eventual consistency has a huge impact on the complexity of the application business logic design. Recent proposals to use transactional causal consistency in serverless computing and microservices seem promising because it reduces the number of possible concurrent execution anomalies that can occur due to the lack of isolation. However, existing tools are technologically complex, making experimentation with complex business logic difficult. We propose a transactional causal consistency simulator to test the behavior of business logic rich microservices applications. It promotes the design of complex business logic transactional causal consistent microservices in a software developer-friendly environment. The simulator is a publicly available artifact that can be reused in other experiments.

Keywords: Microservices · Simulator · Transactional Causal Consistency

1 Introduction

Microservices have become increasingly adopted [14] as the architecture of business systems, because it promotes the split of the domain model into consistent pieces that are owned by small agile development teams and facilitate scalability [7,20].

These systems are implemented using the Saga pattern [17] to handle concurrency anomalies, such as lost update and dirty reads, resulting in extra complexity in the implementation of the system business logic [18]. There is a trade-off between the complexity of business logic and the use of microservices [11]. This is also confirmed by the type of systems where the use of microservices has been successfully reported, where there is the need for high scalability, but the domain business logic is less complex, e.g. Netflix.

This work was partially supported by Fundação para a Ciência e Tecnologia (FCT) through projects UIDB/50021/2020 (INESC-ID) and PTDC/CCI-COM/2156/2021 (DACOMICO). Artifacts available in https://zenodo.org/record/7854925.

M. Patiño-Martínez and J. Paulo (Eds.): DAIS 2023, LNCS 13909, pp. 57–73, 2023.
https://doi.org/10.1007/978-3-031-35260-7_4

Recent research has proposed the use of transactional causal consistency (TCC) to support serverless computing [12,22], which reduces the number of anomalies by providing a causal snapshot to support distributed execution of functionalities. However, to our knowledge, no experimentation with this approach has been carried out with systems that have complex business logic. On the other hand, the two implementations provide a low-level API which is not friendly to the software developer.

The domain-driven concept of aggregate [6] is the basic building block of microservices systems [17], and has been extensively applied by software engineering developers. Therefore, we design and implement a simulator for functionalities that execute according to transactional causal consistency on aggregates. Using the simulator, software engineers can experiment with the design of their TCC microservices systems in a development-friendly environment.

After the introduction, in this section, related work is presented in Sect. 2, and an example that is used throughout the article is described in Sect. 3. Section 4 defines the semantics of the TCC simulator for microservices systems and Sect. 5 its architecture. Section 6 describes how the simulator is used in the running example. Finally, Sect. 7 draws the conclusions.

2   Related Work

The microservice architecture must comply with what is stated by the CAP theorem [9], in particular, there is a trade-off between consistency and availability. Therefore, eventual consistency [2] has been adopted in the implementation of microservices, using sagas [10,17]. However, writing application business logic in the context of eventual consistency requires an extra effort [18] to deal with anomalies such as lost updates and dirty reads. This is due to the intermediate states created by the execution of functionality in each of the microservices. Due to this lack of isolation, the implementation of business logic is intertwined with the handling of the incomplete states. The resulting complexity depends on the number of these intermediate states and the number of functionalities [18].

Therefore, implementing a system using microservices is not trivial. Depending on the complexity of the business logic [11] it may become so complex that it is necessary to migrate the system back to a monolith architecture [13].

Transactional causal consistency [1] has been proposed as a transactional model that handles some of the problems of eventual consistency by providing to the executing functionality a causally-consistent snapshot. The entities in the causal snapshot respect the *happens-before* relation and the writes performed when the functionality commits are atomically visible, regardless of the node in which the read or write operation occurs. This transactional model handles dirty reads because the reads are consistent but continue to allow lost updates, which occur when two concurrent functionalities write the same entity and the last to commit overwrites the first one. On the other hand, TCC can be implemented using non-blocking algorithms, overcoming the limitations stated in the CAP theorem.

There are recent implementations of causal consistency [4,12,21,22], but these implementations use a key-value store and/or offer a low-level API that does not facilitate experimentation with complex business logic using TCC. Additionally, they only use toy cases to experiment with the application of causal consistency.

On the other hand, the design of microservices is based on the domain-driven design concept of aggregate [6,17], which denotes the transactional unit of consistency in microservices. Furthermore, the concept of bounded context [6] is used to divide a domain model and support different perspectives of the same domain element. For instance, person in academic and financial bounded contexts may share some attributes and diverge in other. However, existing TCC implementations do not consider this modeling mechanism, focusing on replica management. There are some synergies between both approaches that are worth exploring but, as far as we know, are not addressed by the literature.

Some research is done on the extension of aggregates to ensure consistency between replicas of entities in data-intensive distributed systems, such as microservices [3]. However, these extensions focus on microservices systems running with eventual consistency. Other relevant works that deal with replica consistency is the research on conflict-free replicated data types [16,23], which use state- and operation-based strategies for replica consistency.

In this paper, we intend to leverage existing work by enriching the concept of aggregate to support TCC semantics. Additionally, we develop a TCC simulator that facilitates experimentation with the implementation of complex microservices systems, applying TCC semantics to the functionalities execution, and doing merging of concurrent changes at the application-semantic level.

3   Running Example

Aggregates are considered the basic building blocks of microservices applications [17]. The concept was imported from domain-driven design [6] and defines a unit of consistency between the aggregate entities, which is defined by the aggregate invariants. An aggregate has a root entity that guarantees atomic accesses, the aggregate entities can only be accessed in the context of its root entity. The root entity defines the lock granularity. Therefore, in the context of microservices, aggregate accesses occur using ACID transactions.

Listing 1.1 presents three aggregates of the Quizzes Tutor application[1]: *Tournament*, *Course*, and *Topic*. Each root entity of the aggregate has a key attribute that is used by other aggregates to refer to it. In the example, the *Tournament* aggregate is built on the *Course* and *Topic* aggregates to define a quiz tournament (not shown), whose questions are about the tournament topics (*topics*). The tournament is created by a student who is enrolled in the course (*creator*) and the course students can participate in the tournament (*participants*).

The aggregate consistency is defined by a set of intra-invariants, specified using a Java Streams like syntax where *root* denotes the aggregate root entity.

---

[1] https://github.com/socialsoftware/quizzes-tutor.

The example shows three intra-invariants of the tournament aggregate: (1) the tournament end is after its start; (2) participants should enroll before the tournament starts; (3) if the creator is also a participant of the tournament, then the value of their name attribute should be the same.

```
Aggregate Tournament {                              Aggregate Course {
  Root Entity Tournament {                            Root Entity Course {
    Integer id key;                                     Integer id key;
    DateTime startTime, endTime;                        List<Student> students;
    Creator creator;                                  }
    List<Topic> topics;                               Entity Student {
    List<Participant> participants;                     Integer number;
  }                                                     String name;
  Entity Creator {                                    }
    Integer number;                                 }
    String name;
  }
  Entity Topic {                                    Aggregate Topic {
    Integer id;                                       Root Entity Topic {
    String name;                                        Integer id key;
  }                                                     String name;
  Entity Participant {                                }
    Integer number;                                 }
    String name;
    DateTime registration;
  }
  IntraInvariants {
    root.startTime < root.endTime;
    root.participants.allMatch(p -> p.registration < root.startTime);
    root.participants.filter(p -> p.number == root.creator.number)
                     .allMatch(p -> p.name == root.creator.name);
  }
}
```

Listing 1.1. Quizzes Tutor Aggregates and Intra-Invariants

Domain-driven design allows one to control the dependencies between aggregates. The upstream-downstream relationship establishes a dependence between development teams: a downstream team is a client of its upstream teams, but the inverse is not possible. This maps to the dependencies in the layered architectural style, where a top layer (downstream) can invoke a lower layer (upstream), but the latter can only send callbacks to the former. In the example, *Tournament* is downstream of *Course* and *Topic*. In addition, a downstream aggregate can replicate data from an upstream aggregate. In the example, *Creator* and *Participant* are *Student* in the *Course* aggregate, whereas tournament *Topic* is defined in the aggregate *Topic*.

Inter-invariants define the consistency between upstream-downstream aggregates.

```
InterInvariants {
  root.creator.number == Student(root.id, root.creator.number).number
             && root.creator.name == Student(root.id, root.creator.number).name;
  root.participants.allMatch(p -> p.number == Student(root.id, p.number).number
             && p.name == Student(root.id, p.number).name);
  root.topics.allMatch(t -> t.name == Topic(t.id).name);
}
```

Listing 1.2. Quizzes Tutor Inter-Invariants

Listing 1.2 presents three inter-invariants between *Tournament* and its upstream aggregates. Inter-invariants are defined in the downstream aggregate, where *Student(root.id,root.creator.number)* denotes the student with the given *number* in the *Course* entity that has the *id* key, and *Topic(t.id)* denotes the topic with the given *id* in the aggregate *Topic*. The first inter-invariant states that should exist a student in the *Course* aggregate corresponding to the tournament *creator* and they have the same name. The second inter-invariant states the same for all *participants*, and the third that the *topics* should exist in the *Topic* aggregate.

Since the communication from upstream to downstream aggregates is done through events, events can be inferred from the inter-invariants. For example, in the example, we can infer that *Course* emits events for student delete and student name update, which are subscribed by the *Tournament* aggregate. The event handling should maintain the inter-invariants (by updating the local copy appropriately).

In the following, two functionalities, which are external interactions with the system, are considered: *UpdateStudentName* and *AddParticipant*. The former only accesses the *Course* aggregate and emits an event that is subscribed by the *Tournament* aggregate. The latter reads the *Course* aggregate to obtain the student information and writes in the *Tournament* aggregate to add student to the *participants* list.

4 Simulator

As introduced in [1], transactional causal consistent transactions read from a causal snapshot, where the snapshot entities are causally consistent, and the transaction write is atomic. In what follows, we specify a simulator that is centralized, but emulates a distributed system supporting TCC. Additionally, due to the restrictions imposed by upstream-downstream communication, we enrich the simulator with the processing of events.

4.1 Achieving Transactional Causal Consistency

To define the semantics of the execution of functionalities in the context of transactional causal consistency, we introduce the concept of version number. Each aggregate has several versions. A is the set of the versions of all aggregates. Given $a \in A$, $a.version$ denotes its version number. Version numbers form a total order, that is, it is possible to compare any two version numbers, $\forall_{a_i,a_j \in A} a_i.version \leq a_j.version \lor a_j.version < a_i.version$. Given an aggregate version, $a \in A$, $a.aggregate$ denotes its aggregate, and $a.versions$ denotes all aggregate versions of aggregate $a.aggregate$. The version number is unique in $a.versions$. Additionally, there is a version number for each execution of functionality f, denoted by $f.version$, and assigned when it starts. It represents the time at which the execution of the functionality starts. It is the number of the last successfully completed functionality incremented by one (the simulator keeps the version number of the last committed functionality). The functionality version number may be changed subsequently, as we describe below. When the functionality commits, it assigns its version number to all the aggregate versions written by the functionality, which corresponds to TCC atomic write. F is the set of all the functionalities executed, and $F.success \subseteq F$ is the subset of the executions of the functionalities that were successfully completed.

A causal snapshot of an executing functionality is a set of aggregates that are causally consistent given the version number of the functionality. Therefore, a causal snapshot of functionality f, denoted by $f.snapshot$, is defined by a set of aggregate versions $f.snapshot \subseteq A$, such that there are not two versions of the same aggregate, $\nexists_{a_i, a_j \in f.snapshot} a_i.aggregate = a_j.aggregate$. In addition, the aggregates in the causal snapshot were not created by a functionality that finished after f started, $a_i.version < f.version$, and it is the most recent version, $\forall_{a_j \in a_i.versions: a_j.version < f.version} a_j.version < a_i.version$.

As an example, consider an aggregate version a which has version number 5, it was written by functionality with version number 5. Also consider two functionalities, f_i and f_j, which start concurrently, when the last functionality successfully completed has 7 as its version number. So, $f_i.version = f_j.version = 8$. Suppose that f_i finishes first and writes a version of a, it will have version number 8. If f_j reads a to its snapshot after f_i finishes, it finds versions 5 and 8, but it will add version 5 because it is the most recent version smaller than 8, to guarantee causality in the snapshot.

4.2   Functionality Execution

The execution of a functionality f in a transactional causal consistent context has the following steps:

1. When functionality f starts, $f.version = max(F.success.version) + 1$, where $F.success.version$ denotes the set of version numbers of all functionalities executions that finished successfully;
2. Whenever an aggregate is read, a version is selected according to the functionality snapshot conditions and added to it, if not already there;
3. Whenever an aggregate is written, a version is selected according to the functionality snapshot conditions and added to it, if not already there. In case the aggregate is being created, it is assigned the functionality version number. $f.written$ denotes the subset of $f.snapshot$ of the written aggregates;
4. When the functionality finishes execution, it proceeds to commit by performing the following actions, and if the process succeeds, the functionality finishes successfully; otherwise, it aborts:
   (a) The written aggregates should preserve the intra-invariants. Considering that $a.intraInv$ denotes a intra-invariants, $\forall_{a \in f.written} \forall_{irv \in a.intraInv} a.irv$, where $a.irv$ denotes the evaluation of the invariant in a version;
   (b) For each aggregate version to be written, obtain, if exists, the most recent version of the same aggregate that was committed by a concurrent functionality, i.e. $\forall_{a_i \in f.written} a_i.toMerge = max_{a.version}\{a_j \in a_i.versions : a_j.version \geq f.version\}$;
   (c) Merge the concurrent versions, denoted by $merge(a_i, a_i.toMerge)$;
   (d) Update the functionality version number to the most recent successfully completed functionality version number plus one, and commit the written aggregates using the new functionality version number, $f.version$.

Transactional causal consistency has the lost update anomaly, which occurs when there are several concurrently executing functionalities updating the same aggregates. Although current TCC implementations do not handle this problem, the design of business logic needs to either abort the last transaction or try to merge it with the most recent committed version.

The merging occurs in two versions of an aggregate, $merge(a_i, a_j)$, where a_i is the version of the functionality to commit and a_j the version already committed. To do the merge, it is necessary to find the version that is the common ancestor of both versions, in order to identify the differences. Since the version to be committed evolved from a committed version, this version is the common ancestor and is denoted by $a_i.prev$. Note that between $a_i.prev$ and a_j can be several other committed versions, if several concurrent functionalities have committed. However, it is possible to identify which attributes were changed compared to the common ancestor, which is denoted, respectively, by $diff(a_i.prev, a_i) \subseteq a.attributes$ and $diff(a_i.prev, a_j) \subseteq a.attributes$, where $a.attributes$ denotes the attributes of $a.aggregate$. Consider the example above, where, instead of two, there are three concurrent functionalities executing with version number 8, f_i, f_j and f_k, and all writing aggregate a. Suppose that f_i finishes first with version number 8, and then f_j with version number 9. When f_k tries to commit its written aggregate a, it finds the aggregate a with version 9. The common ancestor will be version 5, and so the differences will be between versions 5 and 9, and version 5 and the version f_k is trying to write.

The aggregate designer has to define the semantics of consistent merges, which depend on the aggregate semantics. The idea is that the merge should preserve the intention of each one of the functionalities [19]. For instance, suppose that a functionality changes the start and end dates of a tournament and that one user invokes the functionality to change the start date while keeping the end date, and another user concurrently changes the end date while preserving the start date. In this case, it does not make sense to merge the two versions, because it would dismiss the intention of each one of the users, they changed one of the dates while considering the value of the other one. Therefore, the merging can only occur if it does not violate the intention of each one of the functionalities. On the other hand, if a user changes *startTime* and another simultaneously changes *topics*, one of the changes does not violate the other change intention and the merged version contains both.

Therefore, given an aggregate a, the subsets of its attributes that cannot be changed simultaneously in concurrent functionalities are denoted by $a.intentions \subseteq \mathcal{P}(a.attributes)$. For the merge to occur, two attributes concurrently changed cannot be in an intention; otherwise, the functionality has to abort:

$$\forall_{at_i \in diff(a_i.prev, a_i), at_j \in diff(a_i.prev, a_j), at_i \neq at_j} \nexists_{i \in a_i.intentions} : \{at_i, at_j\} \subseteq i$$

The second step of the merge process is to merge the changed attributes, which is done using predefined merge methods defined by the developer. Note that it may not be possible to merge attributes, in which case the merge fails, which is similar to the concept of non-incremental operations defined in the conflict-free data types literature [16]. Therefore, the merge is defined using developer-defined *merge* methods per attribute:

$$\forall_{at \in diff(a_i.prev,a_i) \cap diff(a_i.prev,a_j)} : merge(a_i, a_j, at)$$

In the example, the merging of attributes *startTime* and *endTime* uses the value of the version to be committed (if it was changed). Concerning the attribute *participants*, the change made in the version to be committed is integrated with the change made by the committed version, e.g., a participant is added in each version, and the merged version contains both added participants. On the other hand, the merge of the attribute *topics* uses the value of the version to be committed (if it was changed), because the creator defines the tournament for a concrete set of topics. The difference between the merging of *participants* and *topics* illustrates that the merging semantics is aggregate dependent, even though they are both of type list.

Overall, the process of merging two aggregate versions follows the following steps:

1. Verify intention conditions;
2. Merge the changed attributes;
3. Run intra-invariants in the merged version.

4.3   Event Handling

The transactional model for aggregates has an additional level of complexity due to the upstream-downstream relation between aggregates. Downstream aggregates have to subscribe to the relevant events that are emitted by their upstream aggregates. The set of events that an aggregate version subscribes to is dynamically calculated; it depends on the aggregate version information. In the example, a tournament subscribes the update student name event emitted by the course aggregate events only if the event refers to the creator or one of its participants.

Due to the occurrence of these events, it is necessary to reassess the causal consistency associated with the functionality execution. The causal snapshot associated with functionality execution should also guarantee that all the aggregates subscribing to an event are consistent when involved in a causal transaction, i.e., they have processed all the events in common.

As an example, consider three different aggregate versions a_i, a_j and a_k, where the last two subscribe to the same event as the first one. In a causal snapshot two cases can occur: (1) a_j and a_k belong to the snapshot but a_i does not; (2) a_i and a_j belong to the snapshot. Other cases are similar to or a combination of these two cases. In the first case, it is necessary to ensure that both versions process the events to which they subscribe in common. In the second case, it is necessary to ensure that all events emitted by a_i have been processed by a_j, if it subscribes to them.

Given an event $e \in E$, where E is the set of all events, *e.type* denotes the type of event, *e.aggregate* the aggregate that emits the event, and *e.version* denotes the version of the aggregate that emits the event. Given an aggregate version a, $a.subsEvs \subseteq E$ denotes the events to which it subscribes and $a.emitEvs \subseteq E$ the set of events it has emitted.

An aggregate event subscription is a condition that uses the aggregate version of the event sender and the type of event to identify the subscribed events. The sender aggregate version indicates the last version of the aggregate sender on which the aggregate subscriber depends. Therefore, after an aggregate processes an event, it updates the aggregate version of the event sender. For instance, the tournament subscribes to the update student name event, and it contains the course version to which it subscribes. Note that it is not necessarily the most recent version of course, because the course may have evolved without sending events relevant for the tournament. It can also be the case that the course emitted an event that the tournament has not yet processed. Therefore, the subscriber can process events sent by aggregates that have a higher version number than the version it subscribes to. This is defined in the subscription condition. We also consider that the event publish-subscribe channel is causal order.

Therefore, to handle the impact of eventual consistency in the system, two additional conditions have to be added to the functional causal snapshot.

For the first condition, if two aggregates subscribe to an event of an upstream aggregate and they are in causal snapshot, they should be consistent according to the processing of the event, even if the upstream aggregate is not part of the causal snapshot.

$$\forall_{a_j,a_k \in f.snapshot, a_i \in A} \forall_{e \in a_i.emitEvs}$$
$$e \in a_j.subsEvs \cap a_k.subsEvs \ \lor \ e \notin a_j.subsEvs \cup a_k.subsEvs$$

Therefore, either both subscribe the event and have not processed it, or do not subscribe it, which means that it is already processed or it is not relevant.

The second condition specifies that if upstream and downstream aggregates are in the snapshot, all events emitted by the former must be processed by the latter.

$$\forall_{a_i,a_j \in f.snapshot} \forall_{e \in a_i.emitEvs} \ e \notin a_j.subsEvs$$

If the emitted event does not belong to a_j's subscribed events, it was already processed or is not relevant for a_j.

Events are emitted at functionality commit time to guarantee the atomicity of the creation of the new aggregate version and the emission of the event. The event version is equal to the functionality version that made the change in the aggregate, which is also the aggregate version. Similarly, an event is considered processed when the functionality it triggered commits. An event may be associated with more than one inter-invariant if it depends on the same change of the upstream aggregate, which corresponds, actually, to the update name event that is associated with two inter-invariants.

5   Architecture

The simulator uses an architecture where each functionality is available as a web service, the interactions with the aggregates are done using ACID transactions, which simulate the aggregate atomicity, and the interactions with downstream aggregates are done writing events in a database that is periodically queried by a scheduler. When the event is detected by the scheduler, it is also processed using transactional causal consistency. The *Unit of Work* pattern [8, Chapter 11] is used to implement the transactional causal consistency.

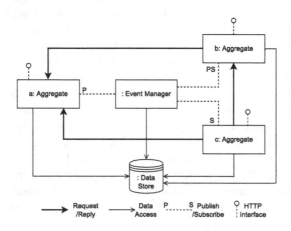

Fig. 1. Simulator: Component-and-Connector View

Figure 1 presents a component-and-connector view [5] of the simulator architecture. It has three component types, *Aggregate*, *Event Manager* and *Data Store*, and four connector types. The request/reply connector implements the upstream-downstream relations between aggregate components, where the invoker is the downstream aggregate. The publish-subscribe connector implements the event channels, which are managed by the *Event Manager* component, and have publish and subscribe roles. For example, the aggregate *b* is both a publisher and a subscriber, because it emits events that are consumed by its downstream aggregate *c* and subscribes events from its upstream aggregate *a*. Aggregate components use data access connectors to manage their aggregates persistence, whereas the event manager component uses the data access connector to persist the events. Finally, the aggregate components have an HTTP interface connector that is used to start its functionalities.

Figure 2 depicts the interactions associated with the execution of a simple functionality of the aggregate *b*, which reads aggregate *c*. The execution, which occurs in the component of the main aggregate, starts by creating a unit of work, that is responsible to manage the causal transaction. The read of aggregates is intercepted by the unit of work that adds the version to the causal snapshot. The changes made to the aggregate *b* are recorded in the unit of work. On commit, the unit of work performs the verifications and required merges, finishing by writing the new version of the aggregate and the events to emit in the data store.

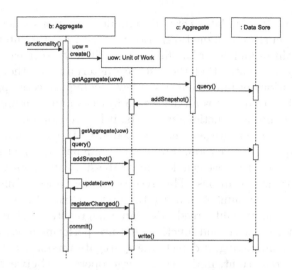

Fig. 2. Simulator: Functionality Interaction

The simulator exercises the causal transactional behavior of the functionality. Each aggregate invocation is performed in a system transaction, which allows interleaving with other executing functionalities. The commit is a serializable transaction which guarantees the atomic write of all versions, where each version is written with the unit of work version number. On the other hand, the events are also written in the commit, which guarantees that their emission and processing are atomic with the aggregate changes.

The processing of events is periodically triggered by the event manager that checks the events in the data store and starts their processing in their own functionality, which executes in a causal transaction transaction. Therefore, during a functionality execution, it is possible that one of the changed aggregates is also changed due to the processing of an event. This situation is detected during the commit and may trigger the merge of the two aggregate versions.

6   Evaluation

To evaluate whether the simulator can implement complex business logic and support the test of complex interleavings, a case study was implemented with 8 aggregates of the Quizzes Tutor application, in a total of 42 functionalities: 14 queries; 24 functionalities that write in a single aggregate; and 4 functionalities that write in two or more aggregates. Due to space limitations, we cover some aspects of the implementation associated with the subset in Listing 1.1, but the complete implementation is available in a public repository.

To verify that the simulator correctly handles situations where concurrency anomalies can occur, we designed scenarios that exercise the interleaved execution of functionalities and event handling. For each of the scenarios, Spock[2] tests were written. To guarantee that the tests are deterministic, though simulating concurrent executions of functionalities, a few techniques were applied.

A functionality that writes an aggregate finishes and commits with version number n. When another functionality starts, it has version number $n+1$, which means that it reads the aggregate version created by the first functionality. This is a standard sequential execution. If we want to simulate a concurrent execution of these two functionalities, we can decrement the simulator kept version number by 1, between their executions. This results in the second functionality also starting with a version number of n like the first, instead of $n + 1$. This ensures that the second functionality reads the same aggregate versions read by the first functionality. If the second functionality also performs a write on the same aggregate, upon committing, it detects the aggregate version written by the first functionality as concurrent, initiating a merge operation between the two. We can decide which concurrent functionality does the merge by running it after the version decrement, after the other has finished.

Another technique was used to handle event detection. Event detection runs periodically at a given frequency, which depends on when the last event handling finished. However, during tests, it is sometimes useful to trigger the event detection at a precise moment in the test, for instance, when trying to test the concurrent execution of an event handling and a functionality. To achieve this, we can block the periodic processing of events and decide when to explicitly trigger the detection and processing of a specific event type for an aggregate.

Figure 3 shows the different interleaving associated with the execution of *updateStudentName* and *addParticipant* functionalities, where the former emits the student name update event. In the scenarios, R, W, P, and E denote, respectively, the read of a version, write a version inside the causal transaction, write a new version (persistent), and emit an event associated with a new version. The functionality and event processing versions correspond to their initial version number. Commits are operations that can span several aggregates and are represented with a vertical line to represent their atomicity.

In Fig. 3a add participant succeeds when it adds the tournament to the causal snapshot, because the event emitted by course is not subscribed by tournament. This occurs because the updated student is not yet a tournament participant. Afterwards, the event is not detected by the tournament because it already contains the updated participant. In Fig. 3b the add participant commits first, and the event processing occurs after both functionalities commit. The event processing changes the participant with the new information, because the tournament subscribes to changes in the course version, 2 to 7, where the student name changed. In Fig. 3c, we illustrate the case where both functionalities execute concurrently and add participant finishes first. Therefore, when the update student finishes, the tournament subscribes to the emitted event. Like in the

---

[2] https://spockframework.org/.

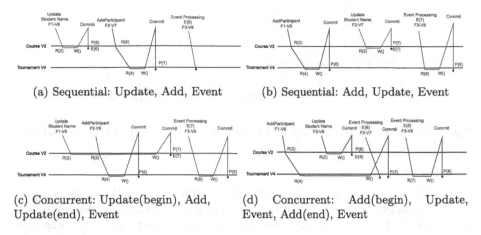

(a) Sequential: Update, Add, Event

(b) Sequential: Add, Update, Event

(c) Concurrent: Update(begin), Add, Update(end), Event

(d) Concurrent: Add(begin), Update, Event, Add(end), Event

Fig. 3. Functionalities and Event Processing Interleaving

previous case, the event processing updates the participant with the new information. Figure 3d illustrates the other concurrent case, where the update student finishes first. In the scenario, the event detection occurs twice. First, it is not detected because tournament version 4 does not contain the student as a participant. The second time is after add participant commits, where tournament subscribes course versions higher than 2, the event is version 6, and the changed student is a participant of tournament version 7.

The following Spock test implements Fig. 3c test case, where the setup creates the course, students, and tournament. The example illustrates the simplicity of a deterministic simulation of a complex concurrent interleaving.

```
def 'concurrent add student and update name; add student finishes first' () {
    given: 'student is added to tournament'
    tournamentFunctionalities.addParticipant(tournamentDto.id, userDto.id)
    and. 'the version number is decreased to simulate concurrency'
    versionService.decrementVersionNumber()
    and: 'student name is updated and the commit does not require merge'
    def updateNameDto = new UserDto()
    updateNameDto.setName(UPDATED_NAME)
    courseFunctionalities.updateStudentName(courseDto.id, userDto.id, updateNameDto)

    when: 'force update name event to be processed'
    tournamentEventDetection.detectUpdateStudentNameEvent();

    then: 'the name is updated in course'
    def courseDtoResult = courseFunctionalities.getCourseByAggregateId(courseDto.id)
    courseDtoResult.students.find{it.id == userDto.id}.name == UPDATED_NAME
    and: 'the name is updated in tournament'
    def tournamentDtoResult = tournamentFunctionalities.findTournament(tournamentDto.id)
    tournamentDtoResult.participants.find{it.id == userDto.id}.name == UPDATED_NAME
}
```

A tournament that has the creator also as a participant subscribes the update name event twice, one to update the creator and the other to update the participant. This corresponds to the first and second inter-invariants of Listing 1.2. A complex interleaving occurs when add participant executes concurrently with update student name, the latter finishes first, and update name event processing is also concurrent with add participant, where add participant finishes first, see Fig. 4.

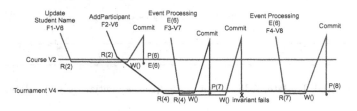

Fig. 4. Concurrent: Update (begin), Add (begin), Update (end), Event (begin), Add (end), Event (abort), Event

In this interaction, add participant adds the student using the previous name, and the event processing only updates the creator name because it uses a previous version of the tournament where the creator is not a participant. So, when the event processing tries to commit, the merge integrates the version where the creator has the updated name with the version where the creator is a participant with the old name. However, the third intra-invariant in Listing 1.1 fails in the merged version and the commit has to abort. In Fig. 4 it is also shown that if the event processing is retried, using the most recent version of the tournament, then the event processing changes the name in both the creator and the participant, and succeeds.

The code for the test case illustrates how this complex interleaving can be exercised in the simulator. Note that when the system version number is decremented, the simulator automatically resets it to its correct value after it is used to start the concurrent functionality.

```
def 'concurrent add creator and update its name: update name finishes first and
        event processing starts before add creator finishes' () {
    given: 'creator name is updated'
    def updateNameDto = new UserDto()
    updateNameDto.setName(UPDATED_NAME)
    courseFunctionalities.updateStudentName(courseDto.id, userCreatorDto.id,
      updateNameDto)
    and: 'the version number is decreased to simulate concurrency'
    versionService.decrementVersionNumber()
    and: 'add creator as participant which uses a previous version of the name,' +
        'creator and participant have the same info'
    tournamentFunctionalities.addParticipant(tournamentDto.id, userCreatorDto.id)
    and: 'the version number is decreased to simulate concurrency'
    versionService.decrementVersionNumber()

    when: 'process update name in the tournament that does not have participant,'+
        'so only the creator is updated, and when merging with the tournament' +
        'that has participant, creator and participant have different names'
    tournamentEventDetection.detectUpdateStudentNameEvent()

    then: 'fails because invariant about same info for creator and participant breaks
      '
    def error = thrown(TutorException)
    error.errorMessage == ErrorMessage.INVARIANT_BREAK
    and: 'process update name event using tournament version that has creator and
      participant'
    tournamentEventDetection.detectUpdateStudentNameEvent();
    and: 'the name is updated in course'
    def courseDtoResult = courseFunctionalities.getCourseByAggregateId(courseDto.id)
    courseDtoResult.students.find{it.id == userCreatorDto.id}.name == UPDATED_NAME
    and: 'the creator is updated in tournament'
    def tournamentDtoResult = tournamentFunctionalities.findTournament(tournamentDto.
      id)
    tournamentDtoResult.creator.name == UPDATED_NAME
    and: 'the creator is participant with updated name'
    tournamentDtoResult.participants.size() == 1
    tournamentDtoResult.participants.find{it.id == userCreatorDto.id}.name ==
      UPDATED_NAME
}
```

6.1 Threats to Validity

To simplify the implementation of transactional causal consistency, we used version numbers to select the aggregates that belong to a causal snapshot. However, in a distributed implementation, the generation of a total order of version numbers is not possible, or at least it does not scale. Nevertheless, TCC [12,22] existing implementations support a similar semantics in the construction of causal snapshots using timestamp intervals. Additionally, the causal snapshot we defined is a best effort snapshot, which in the distributed context may be harder to achieve. Anyway, the transactional semantics and how it impacts on the business logic design is the same.

We are not addressing the replication of aggregates. This problem is usually understood as a low-level data issue, associated with performance. However, we look at it as a higher level of abstraction by defining the inter-invariants, which define consistency rules for the information replicated between two aggregates. This is, in our opinion, the correct way to look at it from a software engineering business logic perspective, because it allows structural variations in the replicated information. There is a software design concern in the replication of information between aggregates.

7 Conclusion

Microservice architectures have to handle the burden of eventual consistency. The Saga pattern has been used to implement the microservices functionalities, but it is well known that there is a trade-off between the amount of application business logic and its implementation effort using a microservices architecture. We leverage on previous works that propose the use of transactional causal consistency in serverless computing to define an approach for the use of TCC on the implementation of microservices business logic, which reduces its implementation complexity. On the other hand, the design and experimentation of a microservice architecture is hindered by the complexity of the infrastructure associated with the distributed communication mechanisms and frameworks. Therefore, it is not easy to experiment with several design possibilities.

We propose a simulator that implements TCC, supporting the concept of aggregate, that is considered the basic building block for the design of microservice architectures. Using the simulator, it is possible to implement complex business logic and experiment design variations. Additionally, a set of test cases can be implemented to evaluate the most complex functionality execution interleavings in a deterministic context. In future work, we intend to use the invariants to automatically generate test cases and analyze the coverage of the automatically generated tests.

The simulator code and a large case study implementation are publicly available at Zenodo [15].

References

1. Akkoorath, D.D., et al.: Cure: strong semantics meets high availability and low latency. In: 2016 IEEE 36th International Conference on Distributed Computing Systems (ICDCS), pp. 405–414 (2016). https://doi.org/10.1109/ICDCS.2016.98
2. Bailis, P., Ghodsi, A.: Eventual consistency today: limitations, extensions, and beyond. Commun. ACM **56**(5), 55–63 (2013)
3. Braun, S., Bieniusa, A., Elberzhager, F.: Advanced domain-driven design for consistency in distributed data-intensive systems. In: Proceedings of the 8th Workshop on Principles and Practice of Consistency for Distributed Data, PaPoC 2021. Association for Computing Machinery, New York (2021). https://doi.org/10.1145/3447865.3457969
4. Bravo, M., Gotsman, A., de Régil, B., Wei, H.: UniStore: a fault-tolerant marriage of causal and strong consistency. In: 2021 USENIX Annual Technical Conference (USENIX ATC 2021), pp. 923–937. USENIX Association (2021). https://www.usenix.org/conference/atc21/presentation/bravo
5. Clements, P., et al.: Documenting Software Architectures: Views and Beyond, 2nd edn. Addison-Wesley, Boston (2011)
6. Evans, E.: Domain-Driven Design: Tackling Complexity in the Heart of Software. Addison Wesley, Boston (2003)
7. Fowler, M.: Microservices. https://martinfowler.com/articles/microservices.html
8. Fowler, M.: Patterns of Enterprise Application Architecture. Addison-Wesley, Boston (2003)
9. Fox, A., Brewer, E.A.: Harvest, yield, and scalable tolerant systems. In: Proceedings of the The Seventh Workshop on Hot Topics in Operating Systems, HOTOS 1999, p. 174. IEEE Computer Society, USA (1999)
10. Garcia-Molina, H., Salem, K.: Sagas. In: Proceedings of the 1987 ACM SIGMOD International Conference on Management of Data, SIGMOD 1987, pp. 249–259. Association for Computing Machinery, New York (1987). https://doi.org/10.1145/38713.38742
11. Haywood, D.: In defense of the monolith. Microservices vs. Monoliths - The Reality Beyond the Hype (2017). https://www.infoq.com/minibooks/emag-microservices-monoliths/
12. Lykhenko, T., Soares, R., Rodrigues, L.: Faastcc: efficient transactional causal consistency for serverless computing. In: Proceedings of the 22nd International Middleware Conference, Middleware 2021, pp. 159–171. Association for Computing Machinery, New York (2021). https://doi.org/10.1145/3464298.3493392
13. Mendonça, N.C., Box, C., Manolache, C., Ryan, L.: The monolith strikes back: why istio migrated from microservices to a monolithic architecture. IEEE Softw. **38**(5), 17–22 (2021). https://doi.org/10.1109/MS.2021.3080335
14. O'Hanlon, C.: A conversation with werner vogels. Queue 4(4), 14–22 (2006). https://doi.org/10.1145/1142055.1142065
15. Pereira, P., Silva, A.R.: socialsoftware/business-logic-consistency-models: v1.0 (2023). https://doi.org/10.5281/zenodo.7854925
16. Preguiça, N., Marques, J.M., Shapiro, M., Letia, M.: A commutative replicated data type for cooperative editing. In: 29th IEEE International Conference on Distributed Computing Systems, ICDCS 2009, pp. 395–403. IEEE (2009). https://doi.org/10.1109/ICDCS.2009.20
17. Richardson, C.: Microservices Patterns. Manning Publications Co., New York (2019)

18. Santos, N., Rito Silva, A.: A complexity metric for microservices architecture migration. In: 2020 IEEE International Conference on Software Architecture (ICSA), pp. 169–178 (2020). https://doi.org/10.1109/ICSA47634.2020.00024
19. Sun, C., Jia, X., Zhang, Y., Yang, Y., Chen, D.: Achieving convergence, causality preservation, and intention preservation in real-time cooperative editing systems. ACM Trans. Comput.-Hum. Interact. **5**(1), 63–108 (1998). https://doi.org/10.1145/274444.274447
20. Thönes, J.: Microservices. IEEE Softw. **32**(1), 116–116 (2015)
21. Toumlilt, I., Sutra, P., Shapiro, M.: Highly-available and consistent group collaboration at the edge with colony. In: Proceedings of the 22nd International Middleware Conference, Middleware 2021, pp. 336–351. Association for Computing Machinery, New York (2021). https://doi.org/10.1145/3464298.3493405
22. Wu, C., Sreekanti, V., Hellerstein, J.M.: Transactional causal consistency for serverless computing. In: Proceedings of the 2020 ACM SIGMOD International Conference on Management of Data, SIGMOD 2020, pp. 83–97. Association for Computing Machinery, New York (2020). https://doi.org/10.1145/3318464.3389710
23. Yu, W., Ignat, C.L.: Conflict-free replicated relations for multi-synchronous database management at edge. In: IEEE International Conference on Smart Data Services, 2020 IEEE World Congress on Services, Beijing, China (2020). http://hal.inria.fr/hal-02983557

The Impact of Importance-Aware Dataset Partitioning on Data-Parallel Training of Deep Neural Networks

Sina Sheikholeslami[1]([⊠])(iD), Amir H. Payberah[1](iD), Tianze Wang[1](iD),
Jim Dowling[1,2](iD), and Vladimir Vlassov[1](iD)

[1] KTH Royal Institute of Technology, Stockholm, Sweden
{sinash,payberah,tianzew,jdowling,vladv}@kth.se
[2] Hopsworks AB, Stockholm, Sweden
jim@hopsworks.ai

Abstract. Deep neural networks used for computer vision tasks are typically trained on datasets consisting of thousands of images, called examples. Recent studies have shown that examples in a dataset are not of equal importance for model training and can be categorized based on quantifiable measures reflecting a notion of "hardness" or "importance". In this work, we conduct an empirical study of the impact of importance-aware partitioning of the dataset examples across workers on the performance of data-parallel training of deep neural networks. Our experiments with CIFAR-10 and CIFAR-100 image datasets show that data-parallel training with importance-aware partitioning can perform better than vanilla data-parallel training, which is oblivious to the importance of examples. More specifically, the proper choice of the importance measure, partitioning heuristic, and the number of intervals for dataset repartitioning can improve the best accuracy of the model trained for a fixed number of epochs. We conclude that the parameters related to importance-aware data-parallel training, including the importance measure, number of warmup training epochs, and others defined in the paper, may be considered as hyperparameters of data-parallel model training.

Keywords: Data-parallel training · Example importance · Distributed deep learning

The authors would like to acknowledge funding from Vinnova for the Digital Cellulose Competence Center (DCC), Diary number 2016-05193. This work has also been partially supported by the ExtremeEarth project funded by European Union's Horizon 2020 Research and Innovation Programme under Grant Agreement No. 825258. The computations for some of the experiments were enabled by resources provided by the National Academic Infrastructure for Supercomputing in Sweden (NAISS) and the Swedish National Infrastructure for Computing (SNIC) at C3SE, partially funded by the Swedish Research Council through grant agreement no. 2022-06725 and no. 2018-05973. Artifacts are available in https://doi.org/10.5281/zenodo.7855247 and https://github.com/ssheikholeslami/importance-aware-data-parallel-training.

© IFIP International Federation for Information Processing 2023
Published by Springer Nature Switzerland AG 2023
M. Patiño-Martínez and J. Paulo (Eds.): DAIS 2023, LNCS 13909, pp. 74–89, 2023.
https://doi.org/10.1007/978-3-031-35260-7_5

1 Introduction

Data-parallel training (DPT) is the current best practice for training deep neural networks (DNNs) on large datasets over several computing nodes (a.k.a. *workers*) [11]. In DPT, the DNN (model) is replicated among the workers, and the training dataset is partitioned and distributed uniformly among them. DPT is an iterative process where in each iteration, each worker trains its model replica on its dataset partition for one epoch. After each iteration, the parameters or gradients of the worker models are aggregated and updated. Then, all workers continue the training using the same updated model replicas. This "vanilla" DPT scheme is shown in Fig. 1.

The dataset partitions in vanilla DPT are constructed by *random partitioning*, i.e., randomly assigning training examples to each partition. However, it is known that not all examples within a training dataset are of equal *importance* for training DNNs [2,3,6,13] meaning that different examples contribute differently to the training process and the performance of the trained model (e.g., its prediction accuracy). Prior works have used example importance to improve DNN training schemes, mainly aiming at reducing the total training time or increasing the performance of the trained models. For example, in *dataset subset search* [3], the goal is to find subset(s) of a given training dataset that can be used to train equally good or more performant models compared to the models trained on the initial dataset. Example importance has also been used for developing more effective sampling algorithms for stochastic gradient descent (SGD) [6], or in active learning for choosing the best examples to label [2].

Contributions. All the above-mentioned solutions are mainly designed for non-distributed model training. In this paper, we study different heuristics to assign examples, based on their importance, to workers in a distributed environment and in DPT. In particular, the contributions of this work are as follows.

- We introduce *importance-aware* DPT, which replaces the random partitioning of the dataset across workers in vanilla DPT, with heuristics that partition the dataset based on some pre-determined notion of example importance, e.g., the average loss value of each example over a number of training epochs.
- We study the effects of the hyperparameters of importance-aware DPT, including different (i) example importance measures and metrics, (ii) partitioning heuristics, and (iii) partitioning intervals, on the quality of the training scheme. Our experiments for image classification tasks on CIFAR-10 and CIFAR-100 datasets demonstrate that importance-aware DPT can outperform vanilla DPT in terms of the best test accuracy achieved by models.

The remainder of this paper is structured as follows. In Sect. 2, we provide the necessary background, including an overview of DPT and a review of some related work. In Sect. 3, we present importance-aware DPT and discuss how it differs from vanilla DPT, which is importance-oblivious. In Sect. 4, we discuss our prototype implementation of importance-aware DPT in PyTorch. In Sect. 5, we present the results of our experimental evaluation of importance-aware DPT.

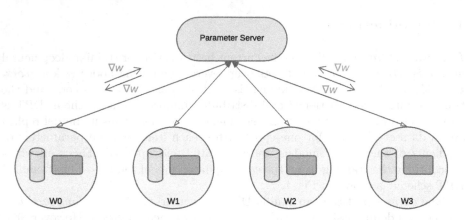

Fig. 1. The vanilla DPT scheme with four workers and one parameter server. At each epoch, each worker gets a random partition of the dataset, and all the workers are assigned the same model replica. After one epoch of training, the workers send their local gradients or model parameters to the parameter server. The parameter server performs either gradient aggregation or model aggregation and sends back the new gradients or parameters to the workers.

Finally, in Sect. 6, we give our conclusions and discuss the current limitations of our importance-aware DPT prototype and further research directions.

2   Background and Related Work

Our work presented in this paper lies in the intersection of data-parallel DNN training and prior work that studies the difference of examples within a dataset in terms of their importance for model training. In this section, we give a brief overview of the DPT of DNNs and some related work on example importance.

2.1   DNN Data-Parallel Training (DPT)

Given a training dataset D consisting of training examples $e \in D$, the aim of training the model M is to optimize model parameters with regards to a cost function, e.g., Mean Squared Error or Binary Cross-Entropy, using an iterative optimization algorithm, e.g., Stochastic Gradient Descent. A training dataset is typically made up of examples of a specific type, such as images, structured data, or sentences. During each *epoch* of training, batches of examples are passed through the model, and model parameters are optimized using the iterative optimization algorithm. To scale out the training process, one can use multiple processing nodes, a.k.a. *workers*, and partition the DNN (for model-parallelism) or the dataset (for DPT) and assign them to the workers to enable parallel training. For our purposes, we define a worker $w \in W$ as a process within a processing node that is allocated exactly one GPU, i.e., each worker corresponds to exactly one GPU in our cluster of processing nodes.

In a typical most common DPT scheme, which we refer to as *vanilla DPT*, the DNN is replicated across the workers. At the beginning of each epoch, the dataset is partitioned uniformly at random into disjoint subsets $p \in P$, such that worker w_i is allocated the partition p_i (dataset partitioning step). More formally, $P = \bigcup_{i=0}^{n-1} p_i$ such that $p_i \cap p_j = \emptyset$ for $i \neq j$; and $p_i \neq \emptyset$ for each i. For simplicity, we assume that the number of examples in the dataset, or $|D|$, is divisible by the number of workers, $n = |W|$; but the approach and results can easily be extended to cases where the assumption does not hold.

During an epoch, each worker independently trains its own replica of the DNN model (local training step) on its own partition p_i. At the end of an epoch, a model synchronization step occurs, e.g., using a parameter server, and the workers get a new identical replica of the model. This process is repeated for a specified budget (e.g., a pre-determined number of epochs) or until a model convergence criterion or performance metric is satisfied. We are interested to see if using a partitioning function, based on notions of example importance, may lead to better results compared to vanilla DPT's random partitioning in terms of the target performance metrics. We define the importance of an example, denoted by Imp, as a mapping of an example to a scalar value:

$$Imp : e \rightarrow \mathbb{R} \tag{1}$$

In practice, to implement Imp, a certain property of the example or the result of its interactions with the model (e.g., the loss generated by the example after a forward pass) is used in combination with an aggregation method (e.g., average, or variance of the losses over a number of epochs).

A partitioning function $PartitioningFunction$ maps the examples to workers to create the set of partitions P, where each worker w_i gets the partition p_i. We are interested in using the output of Imp to construct the $PartitioningFunction$. Example definitions for a $PartitioningFunction$ are explained in Sect. 3.3.

2.2 Prior Work on Example Importance

The diversity of examples in training datasets has attracted increasing attention in recent years and has been exploited to improve the state-of-the-art in domains such as dataset subset search [3,12,13] and sampling for SGD [2,6,13,14].

Chitta et al. [3] propose an ensemble active learning approach for dataset subset selection using ensemble uncertainty estimation. They also show that training classifiers on the subsets obtained in this way leads to more accurate models compared to training on the full dataset. Isola et al. [5] investigate the *memorability* of different examples based on the probability of each image being recognized (perceived as a repetition by the viewer) after a single view and train a predictor for image memorability based on image features. Memorability is also a familiar phenomenon to humans, as we can all think of images or visual memories that have stuck more in our minds compared to other images. Arpit et al. [1] define example difficulty as the average misclassification rate over a number of experiments.

Chang et al. [2] propose to prefer *uncertain* examples for SGD sampling, e.g., the examples that are neither consistently predicted correctly with high confidence nor incorrectly. They use two measures for "example uncertainty": (i) the variance of prediction probabilities and (ii) the estimated closeness between the prediction probabilities and the decision threshold. Yin et al. [14] observe that high similarity between concurrently processed gradients may lead to the speedup saturation and degradation of generalization performance for larger batch sizes and suggest that diversity-inducing training mechanisms can reduce training time and enable using larger batch sizes without the said side effects in distributed training.

Vodrahalli et al. [13] propose an importance measure for SGD sampling based on the gradient magnitude of the loss of each example at the end of training and use this measure to select a subset of the dataset for retraining. This measure can also be used to study the diversity of examples in datasets. Katharopoulos and Fleuret [6] propose an SGD sampling method that favors the more *informative* examples, which they describe as the examples that lead to the biggest changes in model parameters. Toneva et al. [12] propose *forgettability* as an importance measure for dataset examples. A forgettable example is an example that gets classified incorrectly at least once, after its first correct classification, over the course of training. They also suggest that the forgetting dynamics can be used to remove many examples from the base training dataset without hurting the generalization performance of the trained model.

Finally, in the domain of natural language processing, Swayamdipta et al. [10] have investigated the difference in example importance. They introduce *data maps* and calculate two measures for each example: the confidence of the model in the true class and the variability of the confidence across different epochs in a single training run. They then categorize the examples into three categories: *easy-to-learn*, *ambiguous*, and *hard-to-learn*.

3   Importance-Aware DPT

Importance-aware DPT consists of three stages of model training, as shown in Fig. 2. In the first stage, which we refer to as *warmup training*, we train the DNN using vanilla DPT for a number of "warmup" epochs (E_{warmup}). Blocks (1) and (2) in Fig. 2 show the first stage. In the second stage, we calculate the *importance* of each example according to a predefined importance measure, e.g., the average loss value of each example over E_{warmup} training epochs. In the third stage (blocks (3)–(5) in Fig. 2), we continue training using *importance-aware* DPT in several *intervals*. Each interval consists of three steps: (i) dataset partitioning, i.e., assigning examples to partitions based on a *heuristic* and allocating one partition to each worker, (ii) model training, i.e., training the DNN using those fixed partitions for $E_{interval}$ epochs, and (iii) example importance calculation, in which we recalculate and update the importance value of each example for the next interval. In the rest of this section, we discuss importance-aware DPT in more detail.

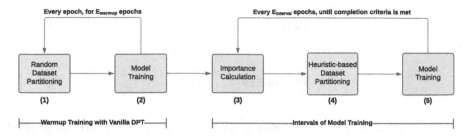

Fig. 2. An overview of Importance-aware data-parallel training. The model is first trained with Vanilla DPT for E_{warmup} epochs, after which the random dataset partitioning is replaced with heuristic-based dataset partitioning, and the dataset is partitioned at the beginning of each interval of training rather than at the beginning of each epoch.

3.1   Warmup Training

In the first stage, warmup training, the model is trained with vanilla DPT for E_{warmup} epochs, in which the dataset is randomly partitioned among the workers at the beginning of each epoch. We collect the value(s) needed for calculating the importance of examples during this stage. In this work, we use the loss value (the result of backpropagation forward pass) of each example in each epoch to calculate its importance value, which is the average loss over a number of epochs. It is worth noting that we will discard the loss values from the first E_{ignore} epochs in warmup training (e.g., the first three epochs), as the losses generated in the first few epochs are influenced by the random initialization of the neural network to a high degree.

3.2   Importance Calculation

The second stage is a pause in model training, in which we calculate the importance of examples using values collected during warmup training. To demonstrate how this works, consider we calculate the importance of each example using "average loss across epochs". To do this, during warmup training, we collect the loss values (the result of the forward pass) of each example across E_{warmup} epochs. At the end of warmup training, we will have a matrix such as in Fig. 3. In this matrix, each row corresponds to a single example, and each column corresponds to an epoch. Hence, an element $a_{i,j}$ in the matrix is the loss value of example i in epoch j. Calculating the importance of each example would then require a simple aggregation or computation over each row, e.g., a row-wise average. At the end of this stage, we have one or more scalar values attributed to each example, indicating its importance, which we use for sorting or categorizing the examples in the next stage (dataset partitioning).

$$\begin{bmatrix} 2.4630 & 1.6089 & ... & 0.8972 \\ ... & ... & ... & ... \\ ... & ... & ... & ... \\ ... & ... & ... & ... \\ 0.9879 & 3.1874 & ... & 1.7276 \end{bmatrix}$$

Fig. 3. example-epoch-loss matrix that is used to calculate the importance score of each example.

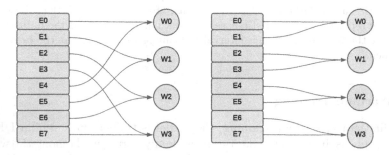

Fig. 4. Depiction of Stripes (left) and Blocks (right) partitioning heuristics for a setting with eight examples (indexed in order of importance) and four workers.

3.3   Dataset Partitioning Heuristics

Now that we have a mapping between examples and their importance values, we can use various heuristics to proceed with dataset partitioning for importance-aware DPT. Remind that in vanilla DPT, the examples are partitioned randomly across the parallel workers at the beginning of each epoch. We have defined two such heuristics, namely Stripes and Blocks, and compared them with random partitioning (i.e., vanilla DPT).

Stripes Heuristic. The Stripes partitioning heuristic is a cyclic assignment of examples to workers. The intuition behind using this heuristic is to preserve the same distribution of examples with regard to their importance values, in each partition. To this end, we sort the examples of the dataset D by their importance value and create a list called *Sorted Examples* (SE). Then, the partition P_i that is allocated to worker w_i is determined as:

$$P_i = \{e \in D \mid sorted\_index(e) \equiv i(\mod n)\} \tag{2}$$

where $sorted\_index(e)$ returns the index of example e in the sorted list SE, n is the number of workers, and $i = 0, ..., n-1$. The Stripes heuristic is depicted on the left side of Fig. 4.

Blocks Heuristic. This partitioning heuristic assigns a continuous block of examples to each worker so that we will end up with different importance distributions across the workers. Assuming n workers, the `Blocks` heuristic allocates the first $\frac{|D|}{n}$ examples ranked in the SE list to the first worker, the second $\frac{|D|}{n}$ of SE to the second worker, and so on. Thus, the partition P_i that is allocated to worker w_i using the `Blocks` heuristic is determined as follows:

$$P_i = \{e \in D \mid i \times \frac{|D|}{n} \leq sorted\_index(e) < (i+1) \times \frac{|D|}{n}\} \qquad (3)$$

where $sorted\_index(e)$ returns the index of example e in the sorted list SE and $i = 0, ..., n-1$. The `Blocks` heuristic is depicted on the right side of Fig. 4.

3.4 Intervals of Model Training

After warmup training, calculating example importance, and partitioning the dataset based on the importance values, we continue model training using fixed partitions in intervals, each comprising of $E_{interval}$ epochs. At the beginning of each training interval, we repartition the dataset using the importance values calculated during the previous interval. This means that dataset repartitioning only occurs at the beginning of each interval rather than at the beginning of every epoch (as in vanilla DPT).

4 Implementation in PyTorch

This section presents the implementation details of importance-aware data-parallel training in PyTorch v1.10.1 [8,9]. The implementation is mainly based on several classes and methods that (i) track and calculate the importance of examples as explained in Sects. 3.1 and 3.2, (ii) partition the dataset across workers based on importance-aware heuristics defined in Sect. 3.3, and (iii) resume and continue the model training for fixed intervals of $E_{interval}$ epochs as described in Sect. 3.4.

4.1 Importance Calculation

Our proof-of-concept implementation of importance-aware DPT provides importance calculation for each example based on its average forward pass loss across a number of epochs. Loss function implementations in PyTorch, by default, do a batch-wise reduction on the losses and return a scalar aggregate value (e.g., the average loss of examples in the mini-batch when using `CrossEntropyLoss`[1]). To get individual (per example) loss values, we construct an additional loss function of the same type and set its `reduction` parameter to `None`. This way, this loss function returns a tensor instead of a scalar.

---

[1] As described in https://pytorch.org/docs/stable/generated/torch.nn.CrossEntropy Loss.html.

Hence, each step of the training consists of two forward passes: the first one uses the customized loss function and writes values to a local worker copy of a loss-epochs matrix similar to the one depicted in Fig. 3, and the second forward pass uses the default loss function implementation which is used with the backward pass. Each worker maintains its own copy of the loss-epochs matrix, and before each dataset partitioning step, the workers wait at a barrier (by calling `torch.distributed.barrier()`) for the main process to merge the local copies and aggregate, i.e., to compute the row-wise average which is the average loss of each example across the epochs. The output of this step is a sorted list of tuples (`example, importance value`) - the *Sorted Examples* list introduced in Sect. 3.3, that is used with the importance-aware partitioning heuristics.

4.2   Dataset Partitioning Heuristics

In PyTorch, the `DistributedDataSampler` class implements the logic for assigning examples to workers. By default, this class contains an implementation of random sampling, so we extend this class and add a sampler, called `ConstantSampler`, to arbitrarily assign the examples to workers. In this way, we decouple the implementation for assigning examples to workers, from the implementation of importance-aware partitioning heuristics. Hence, the same `ConstantSampler` can be used with different partitioning heuristics.

A dataset partitioning heuristics provides a mapping between examples and workers. We implement this mapping in PyTorch by creating a dictionary (`dict`) with worker indices as keys and a list of example indices as the value of each key. Depending on the heuristic, filling in this dictionary would then require iterating over the list of examples or workers. The result of this step, which is a `dict` that maps examples to workers, is used to construct a `ConstantSampler` instance that assigns the dataset examples across the workers. Once the `ConstantSampler` instance is constructed, the main process also reaches the barrier, so all the worker processes exit the barrier they had entered before merging their local matrices (as described in the previous section).

4.3   Modified Training Loop for Importance-Aware Training

Model training in PyTorch typically consists of a few blocks of code for setting up the training (e.g., downloading the dataset, constructing the train/test/validation folds and data samplers, and creating the model), followed by a single loop for iterative training of the model. To implement different stages of importance-aware DPT, we first break down the default training loop into two separate loops: one for warmup training (Sect. 3.1) and the other for intervals of importance-aware training (Sect. 3.4). The first loop is similar to a typical PyTorch training loop but is extended with code to track and calculate the importance of examples. The second loop is nested: an outer loop maintains the intervals, while the inner loop contains the code for the actual dataset partitioning step, the example importance calculation step, and the model training step.

5   Evaluation

In this section, we describe our experimental setup and scenarios and discuss the results of the experiments. When talking about "model performance" we mainly refer to *best test accuracy* of a model trained for 100 epochs. Our hardware setup consists of a single machine with 4 GeForce RTX 2070 SUPER graphic cards, so we train on 4 workers.

5.1   Experimental Setup

To be able to empirically evaluate the effects of importance-aware dataset partitioning on the performance of DPT systems, we use two well-known DNN architectures for image classification: ResNet-18 and ResNet-34 [4] and train them on CIFAR-10 and CIFAR-100 datasets [7]. We use official PyTorch implementations of the models[2] and initialize them with random weights. In total, our experiments consist of 1830 training runs across 183 workloads (different combinations of datasets, models, partitioning heuristics, importance metrics, E_{warmup}, and $E_{interval}$). Three of these 183 workloads use vanilla DPT (ResNet-18 on CIFAR-10, ResNet-34 on CIFAR-10, and ResNet-34 on CIFAR-100), and we use them as baselines for comparison. For all runs that use importance-aware DPT, we set E_{ignore} to 5. We use the same hyperparameters for all runs of vanilla DPT and importance-aware DPT, i.e., SGD with a 0.9 Nesterov momentum and a learning rate starting at 0.1 and weight decay (L2 penalty) of 0.0005.

Considerations for Randomness: The training process of DNNs is a stochastic one and is affected by many factors, e.g., choice of hyperparameters, stochasticity in the optimization algorithms, and the stochastic behavior of the tools, frameworks, and hardware used for training [15]. To better control for this stochasticity, each of the 183 workloads is repeated ten times using ten predetermined global random seeds. In Tables 1, 2, 3, 4 and 5, we report the average best test accuracy and standard deviation of ten runs for each workload. Also, the box plot of the performance of the top five settings of each table, alongside the performance of the corresponding baseline (vanilla DPT), is shown in Fig. 5.

5.2   Different Dataset Complexities

We consider workloads of (ResNet-34, `Stripes`, Variance) with each of the CIFAR-10 and CIFAR-100 datasets. The results of the runs can be seen in Tables 4 and 5, and in Fig. 5 subfigures (4)–(5). CIFAR-10 and CIFAR-100 contain the same number of examples in train (50000 examples) and test (10000 examples) subsets, but they differ in the number of classes. CIFAR-10 has ten classes (5000 training examples per class), and CIFAR-100 has 100 classes (500 training examples per class). Hence, CIFAR-100 has a higher complexity than CIFAR-10 in terms of classes.

---

[2] See https://pytorch.org/vision/main/models.html.

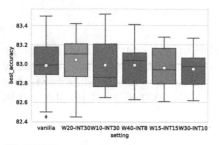

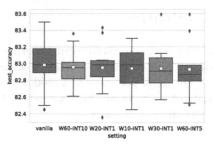

(1) CIFAR-10, ResNet-18, Stripes, Variance (2) CIFAR-10, ResNet-18, Stripes, Average

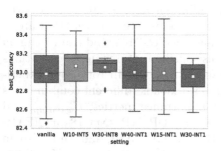

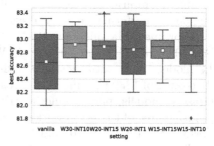

(3) CIFAR-10, ResNet-18, Blocks, Variance (4) CIFAR-10, ResNet-34, Stripes, Variance

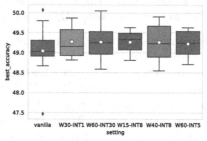

(5) CIFAR-100, ResNet-34, Stripes, Variance

Fig. 5. Box plots comparing the performance of the top 5 settings of E_{warmup} (W) and $E_{interval}$ (INT) for different combinations of (Dataset, Model, Partitioning Heuristic, Importance Metric). The leftmost box plot in each subfigure is the performance of vanilla DPT (baseline), and the other five box plots are ordered in decreasing average best test accuracy. The white square on each box plot denotes the average best test accuracy for a setting. Each subfigure (1)–(5) corresponds to a table with the same number, which contains the average best test accuracies and standard deviations over ten runs for each of the combinations of W and INT.

Table 1. Average best test accuracies (over ten runs) and standard deviations for different combinations of E_{warmup} (W) and $E_{interval}$ (I), when training ResNet-18 on CIFAR-10 with Stripes policy and loss variance as the importance metric. The baseline (using vanilla DPT) is 82.983 ± 0.327.

W	I					
	1	5	8	10	15	30
10	82.766 ± 0.185	82.848 ± 0.278	82.742 ± 0.152	82.862 ± 0.237	82.836 ± 0.387	82.988 ± 0.299
15	82.743 ± 0.373	82.752 ± 0.157	82.891 ± 0.302	82.888 ± 0.296	82.958 ± 0.247	82.873 ± 0.262
20	82.776 ± 0.243	82.832 ± 0.262	82.749 ± 0.309	82.722 ± 0.221	82.878 ± 0.283	83.044 ± 0.311
30	82.846 ± 0.202	82.858 ± 0.376	82.837 ± 0.263	82.946 ± 0.204	82.843 ± 0.307	82.773 ± 0.266
40	82.946 ± 0.246	82.773 ± 0.208	82.985 ± 0.238	82.869 ± 0.364	82.815 ± 0.296	82.827 ± 0.161
60	82.813 ± 0.283	82.898 ± 0.300	82.882 ± 0.152	82.764 ± 0.293	82.830 ± 0.249	82.705 ± 0.415

Table 2. Average best test accuracies (over ten runs) and standard deviations for different combinations of E_{warmup} (W) and $E_{interval}$ (I), when training ResNet-18 on CIFAR-10 with Stripes policy and average loss as the importance metric. The baseline (using vanilla DPT) is 82.983 ± 0.327.

W	I					
	1	5	8	10	15	30
10	82.941 ± 0.262	82.880 ± 0.339	82.859 ± 0.312	82.815 ± 0.290	82.836 ± 0.226	82.891 ± 0.195
15	82.885 ± 0.231	82.816 ± 0.287	82.841 ± 0.316	$82.778 + 0.259$	82.866 ± 0.260	82.773 ± 0.247
20	82.952 ± 0.314	82.913 ± 0.247	82.903 ± 0.240	82.889 ± 0.265	82.841 ± 0.278	82.919 ± 0.210
30	82.939 ± 0.294	82.854 ± 0.185	82.853 ± 0.236	82.889 ± 0.227	82.743 ± 0.335	82.929 ± 0.279
40	82.864 ± 0.138	82.903 ± 0.152	82.883 ± 0.225	82.766 ± 0.220	82.905 ± 0.244	82.851 ± 0.236
60	82.908 ± 0.337	82.931 ± 0.339	82.818 ± 0.245	82.956 ± 0.228	82.806 ± 0.195	82.758 ± 0.237

The results show that there are several combinations of $(E_{warmup}, E_{interval})$ for training settings that can train better models than vanilla DPT. Thus, the gains of importance-aware DPT seem to hold across different datasets, given that we can find and select good hyperparameters for the training setting (e.g., E_{warmup} and $E_{interval}$).

5.3 Different Models

We consider workloads of (CIFAR-10, Stripes, Variance) with each of the ResNet-18 (18 layers, 8 residual blocks) and ResNet-34 (34 layers, 16 residual blocks) models [4]. The results of the runs can be seen in Tables 1 and 4, and in Fig. 5 subfigures (1) and (4). There are combinations of $(E_{warmup}, E_{interval})$ corresponding to each model that train better models than their corresponding baselines, but ResNet-34 shows to gain more from importance-aware DPT than ResNet-18.

Table 3. Average best test accuracies (over ten runs) and standard deviations for different combinations of E_{warmup} (W) and $E_{interval}$ (I), when training ResNet-18 on CIFAR-10 with `Blocks` policy and loss variance as the importance metric. The baseline (using vanilla DPT) is 82.983 ± 0.327.

W	I					
	1	5	8	10	15	30
10	82.921 ± 0.352	83.067 ± 0.270	82.778 ± 0.426	82.743 ± 0.218	82.662 ± 0.240	82.706 ± 0.165
15	82.992 ± 0.321	82.899 ± 0.308	82.890 ± 0.253	82.805 ± 0.165	82.664 ± 0.178	82.109 ± 0.338
20	82.845 ± 0.292	82.939 ± 0.376	82.850 ± 0.429	82.716 ± 0.205	82.747 ± 0.289	82.523 ± 0.165
30	82.956 ± 0.189	82.942 ± 0.309	83.055 ± 0.153	82.954 ± 0.382	82.815 ± 0.247	82.583 ± 0.206
40	83.001 ± 0.270	82.861 ± 0.336	82.786 ± 0.247	82.925 ± 0.18	82.865 ± 0.177	82.894 ± 0.254
60	82.918 ± 0.348	82.873 ± 0.283	82.848 ± 0.271	82.886 ± 0.273	82.884 ± 0.228	82.462 ± 0.222

Table 4. Average best test accuracies (over ten runs) and standard deviations for different combinations of E_{warmup} (W) and $E_{interval}$ (I), when training ResNet-34 on CIFAR-10 with `Stripes` policy and loss variance as the importance metric. The baseline (using vanilla DPT) is 82.661 ± 0.478.

W	I					
	1	5	8	10	15	30
10	82.650 ± 0.547	82.653 ± 0.399	82.590 ± 0.395	82.621 ± 0.243	82.751 ± 0.461	82.753 ± 0.632
15	82.537 ± 0.332	82.424 ± 0.510	82.745 ± 0.401	82.799 ± 0.481	82.832 ± 0.239	82.433 ± 1.020
20	82.845 ± 0.441	82.659 ± 0.637	82.787 ± 0.407	82.606 ± 0.541	82.890 ± 0.321	82.492 ± 0.300
30	82.671 ± 0.434	82.539 ± 0.307	82.719 ± 0.509	82.920 ± 0.287	82.594 ± 0.434	82.720 ± 0.589
40	82.669 ± 0.426	82.773 ± 0.403	82.422 ± 0.728	82.530 ± 0.305	82.649 ± 0.339	82.562 ± 0.353
60	82.789 ± 0.336	82.615 ± 0.342	82.683 ± 0.397	82.768 ± 0.525	82.678 ± 0.451	82.622 ± 0.661

5.4 Different Partitioning Heuristics

We consider workloads of (CIFAR-10, ResNet-18, Variance) with each of the `Stripes` and `Blocks` heuristics. The results of the runs can be seen in Tables 1 and 3, and in Fig. 5 subfigures (1) and (3).

The results show that for both heuristics, there are combinations of $(E_{warmup}, E_{interval})$ that can train better models than vanilla DPT. It is particularly interesting that training using the `Blocks` heuristic shows comparable performance to training with both `Stripes` heuristic and vanilla DPT.

5.5 Different Importance Metrics

With the loss values generated by each example in forward passes across several epochs as our importance measure, we evaluate the effects of the choice of two different metrics: *average loss* and *loss variance*. We consider workloads of (CIFAR-10, ResNet-18, `Stripes`) with each of the above metrics. The results of the runs can be seen in Tables 1 and 2, and in Fig. 5 subfigures (1)–(2). Loss variance as an importance metric performs marginally better than the average loss.

Table 5. Average best test accuracies (over ten runs) and standard deviations for different combinations of E_{warmup} (W) and $E_{interval}$ (I), when training ResNet-34 on CIFAR-100 with **Stripes** policy and loss variance as the importance metric. The baseline (using vanilla DPT) is 49.042 ± 0.698.

W	I					
	1	5	8	10	15	30
10	49.169 ± 0.335	49.064 ± 0.312	49.167 ± 0.432	48.758 ± 0.597	49.04 ± 0.503	49.033 ± 0.450
15	49.156 ± 0.332	48.959 ± 0.437	49.264 ± 0.292	49.186 ± 0.498	49.073 ± 0.573	49.079 ± 0.351
20	48.978 ± 0.550	49.144 ± 0.637	49.024 ± 0.365	49.149 ± 0.297	48.944 ± 0.436	48.977 ± 0.380
30	49.278 ± 0.399	48.906 ± 0.792	49.102 ± 0.393	48.897 ± 0.432	49.152 ± 0.446	48.966 ± 0.389
40	49.129 ± 0.549	48.978 ± 0.527	49.262 ± 0.489	49.155 ± 0.387	48.998 ± 0.450	49.024 ± 0.284
60	49.083 ± 0.348	49.224 ± 0.338	49.027 ± 0.453	49.194 ± 0.396	49.107 ± 0.461	49.270 ± 0.429

Table 6. Overhead statistics (in seconds) of importance-aware DPT when training ResNet-18 on CIFAR-10 with the different 36 combinations of E_{warmup} and $E_{interval}$.

Quantity	Min	Average	Max
Importance tracking overhead (each epoch)	0.979	1.052	1.407
Heuristic overhead (each interval)	2.456	2.643	5.213
Total training time	715	721.556	758

5.6 Added Overheads

The overheads of importance-aware DPT compared to vanilla DPT include (1) tracking importance data for each example at every epoch (a.k.a., importance tracking overhead) and (2) calculating the importance of examples and repartitioning the dataset based on heuristics at the beginning of each interval (a.k.a., heuristic overhead). In Table 6, we report the statistics on these overheads (in seconds) when we train ResNet-18 on CIFAR-10 for 100 epochs using four workers and the different 36 combinations of E_{warmup} and $E_{interval}$ (as reported in Tables 1, 2, 3, 4 and 5). The importance tracking overhead is independent of E_{warmup} and $E_{interval}$, as it happens at every epoch, and on average accounts for 14.57% of the total wallclock time. However, we should note that this is a prototype implementation of importance-aware DPT, and many optimizations can be made to significantly reduce the overheads (e.g., getting the individual example losses and the mini-batch losses in the same forward pass or using MPI operations for calculating the importance of examples). By only requiring repartitioning at every $E_{interval}$, importance-aware DPT has the potential to significantly reduce the network and I/O overhead that vanilla DPT requires for fetching examples at each epoch, especially in large training settings consisting of hundreds of thousands or millions of examples.

6 Conclusion

In this paper, we proposed importance-aware DPT, a data-parallel training approach for deep neural networks, that partitions the dataset examples across the
workers based on a notion of the importance of each example. Our empirical
evaluation across a number of well-known image classification workloads suggests that by setting relevant values for the hyperparameters of this approach,
most notably E_{warmup} and $E_{interval}$, we can find better models (in terms of
best test accuracy) compared to when training with vanilla DPT. Future work
can concentrate on, e.g., using hyperparameter tuning methods for finding the
best values for the hyperparameters of importance-aware DPT and evaluating
the effects of different importance metrics and measures.

References

1. Arpit, D., et al.: A closer look at memorization in deep networks. In: International
   Conference on Machine Learning, pp. 233–242. PMLR (2017)
2. Chang, H.S., Learned-Miller, E., McCallum, A.: Active bias: training more accurate
   neural networks by emphasizing high variance samples. In: Advances in Neural
   Information Processing Systems, vol. 30 (2017)
3. Chitta, K., Alvarez, J.M., Haussmann, E., Farabet, C.: Training data distribution
   search with ensemble active learning. arXiv preprint arXiv:1905.12737 (2019)
4. He, K., Zhang, X., Ren, S., Sun, J.: Deep residual learning for image recognition. In:
   Proceedings of the IEEE Conference on Computer Vision and Pattern Recognition,
   pp. 770–778 (2016)
5. Isola, P., Xiao, J., Parikh, D., Torralba, A., Oliva, A.: What makes a photograph
   memorable? IEEE Trans. Pattern Anal. Mach. Intell. **36**(7), 1469–1482 (2013)
6. Katharopoulos, A., Fleuret, F.: Not all samples are created equal: deep learning
   with importance sampling. In: International Conference on Machine Learning, pp.
   2525–2534. PMLR (2018)
7. Krizhevsky, A.: Learning multiple layers of features from tiny images. Technical
   report, University of Toronto (2009)
8. Li, S., et al.: PyTorch distributed: experiences on accelerating data parallel training. Proc. VLDB Endow. **13**(12), 3005–3018 (2020)
9. Paszke, A., et al.: PyTorch: an imperative style, high-performance deep learning
   library. In: Advances in Neural Information Processing Systems, vol. 32 (2019)
10. Swayamdipta, S., et al.: Dataset cartography: mapping and diagnosing datasets
    with training dynamics. In: Proceedings of the 2020 Conference on Empirical Meth-
    ods in Natural Language Processing (EMNLP), pp. 9275–9293 (2020)
11. Tang, Z., Shi, S., Chu, X., Wang, W., Li, B.: Communication-efficient distributed
    deep learning: a comprehensive survey. arXiv preprint arXiv:2003.06307 (2020)
12. Toneva, M., Sordoni, A., des Combes, R.T., Trischler, A., Bengio, Y., Gordon, G.J.:
    An empirical study of example forgetting during deep neural network learning. In:
    ICLR (2019)
13. Vodrahalli, K., Li, K., Malik, J.: Are all training examples created equal? An
    empirical study. arXiv preprint arXiv:1811.12569 (2018)

14. Yin, D., Pananjady, A., Lam, M., Papailiopoulos, D., Ramchandran, K., Bartlett, P.: Gradient diversity: a key ingredient for scalable distributed learning. In: International Conference on Artificial Intelligence and Statistics, pp. 1998–2007. PMLR (2018)
15. Zhuang, D., Zhang, X., Song, S., Hooker, S.: Randomness in neural network training: characterizing the impact of tooling. In: Marculescu, D., Chi, Y., Wu, C. (eds.) Proceedings of Machine Learning and Systems, vol. 4, pp. 316–336 (2022)

Distributed Architectures

Runtime Load-Shifting of Distributed Controllers Across Networked Devices

Angelo Filaseta and Danilo Pianini[✉]

Alma Mater Studiorum—Università di Bologna, 47522 Cesena, (FC), Italy
angelo.filaseta@studio.unibo.it, danilo.pianini@unibo.it

Abstract. The ability to monitor and steer the behaviour of complex distributed systems is an increasingly hot research topic, fostered by the growing adoption of hybrid cloud-edge technologies that constitute a computational continuum. One key feature of these systems is the ability to scale in size, embracing a wide number of heterogeneous devices and applications. This complexity, in turn, impacts the monitoring and control systems that need, at the same time, to be able to deal with high complexity and computational load and be available on all kinds of devices. In this paper, we introduce an architecture that allows for shifting the computational load of monitor systems at runtime across different devices in the cloud-edge continuum. We show the feasibility of the proposed approach by providing a reference implementation integrated with an existing simulation platform, leveraging Kotlin multiplatform to allow interoperability among different runtimes.

Keywords: Runtime load-shift · Distributed Monitoring · Distributed control · Interoperability

1 Introduction

Recent trends in the development of distributed systems are pushing towards constructing a cloud-edge continuum, where services can migrate opportunistically across very diverse devices [19]. Monitoring and controlling the behaviour of such systems is paramount [7], and although initial studies on distributed monitoring exist [3], it is often achieved by aggregating the information provided by the devices in a sub-portion of the system (often, a single monitoring service) [28]. One problem in this context is the computational load of the monitoring service: if the system is large and complex, it may need to perform heavy-duty computations, such as rendering the relations among the monitored system's components. The problem is exacerbated by the fact that the monitoring/control service must be available on any device an administrator may have access to, hereby including low-power and battery-equipped devices such as smartphones, which may not be able to perform the required computations (or may do so

Artifacts available in https://zenodo.org/record/7817433.

an unacceptable cost in battery life). In general, the monitoring/control service must be able to use the available resources efficiently: if the monitoring device is powerful enough, it can host the computation, freeing the shared resource from the duty; otherwise, it should delegate the computation to a more suitable device. Crucially, the monitoring service must be able to do so at runtime, as the availability of devices may change over time, as well as the actual resource availability; for example, a smartphone kept under charge may well take care of the whole computation, but as soon as it gets disconnected from the power grid, battery consumption concerns apply. Similar considerations can be made for other performance metrics, such as networking issues: mobile devices may be located where the network connectivity is poor, and thus switch at runtime into an operation mode that optimises for low data rate.

Contribution. In this paper, we propose an *architecture* that allows for shifting the computational load of monitoring and control systems *at runtime*. It requires the capability to identify in advance the components that may be moved across devices, and a shared technology or runtime that can execute on all the devices that might need to host the heavy-duty part of the monitoring: consequently, technologies capable of targeting *multiple runtimes* through *multi-target compilation* are particularly well-suited to implement the proposed system.

The remainder of this manuscript is as follows: Sect. 2 introduces the problem we are addressing and shows examples from the industry; Sect. 3 describes the architecture we propose to tackle the problem; Sect. 4 describes a proof-of-concept implementation of the proposed architecture; Sect. 5 exercises the proof-of-concept and draws lessons on the architecture; Sect. 6 concludes the paper and outlines future work.

2   Problem Statement

Consider a (possibly large) distributed system composed of multiple devices and processes that needs to be monitored (namely, information on the system's state needs to be collected, aggregated, and displayed on a monitoring device, generating a directional information flow) and controlled (which, in addition to monitoring the system, can act on it, generating a bidirectional information flow). Assume that the system is monitored and controlled by a single service, which can equivalently be a single process hosted on a single device or a distributed system, as far as it exposes a single entry point. Note that this definition is loose enough to include atypical monitoring and control systems such as simulators, which are often used as development and debugging support when the system is being built. Assume the monitoring/control service to have a hefty computational load in some of its parts; although no specific kind of computation is assumed, a typical example can be the rendering of the relations among the monitored system's components, which may involve the computation of and organisation in space of large graphs whose edges are frequently reshaped (e.g., if the system includes mesh-networked parts and/or mobile devices) and whose node set evolves in time (e.g., if the system is open and new nodes join or leave).

Finally, the monitoring service must efficiently use the available resources on any device an administrator may have access to, ranging from well-equipped workstations to low-power devices such as smartphones (or even more resource-constrained devices, including wearables such as smartwatches). Consequently, the monitoring service must be able to *dynamically* shift its computational load across different devices, balancing the load considering the available resources and the current needs of the system, and supporting scenarios such as *moving the computationally expensive part* on or off a handheld device when the device is connected to the power grid or disconnected from it. To achieve the result, the system needs a state transfer protocol to be in place for the reconfiguration to happen at runtime; different algorithms come with their own properties and guarantees, which the system will inherit. In this work, we focus on the software architecture of the overall load-shifting service, leaving the specific state transfer protocol out of the scope of this contribution.

2.1 Analogies with Systems in the Literature and in the Industry

The idea of moving the computational load of a distributed system across nodes is not new. In particular, *load balancing* is a hot theme [2] in cloud systems, where tasks must be allocated to the available resources in a way that optimises for the system's performance [20]. However, in most cases, tasks running in the cloud are not designed to be portable to the network leaves: load balancing in this context happens at the level of the cloud provider, with certain guarantees of homogeneity (often obtained through virtualisation) [18]. An interesting take on the subject has been proposed by the community working on agent-based programming. Mobile agents are indeed designed to be portable across devices, however, the proposed solutions typically rely on a *shared runtime* or *middleware* capable of executing the agents' specifications [5,6,9]. In this work, we try instead to provide an architecture that allows for shifting the computational load across diverse runtimes.

The problem at hand is akin to systems existing in industry, except that, to the best of our knowledge, none supports dynamic relocation of the heavy-duty part across the edge-cloud continuum. The problem of load-shifting is already relevant and visible by non-expert observers in the videogame industry: from the right abstraction level, a videogame is a controller/monitor of a virtual world whose evolution requires complex logic and audio-video elaboration.

As per many load-intensive applications, the traditional way to play high-end videogames is to use (powerful) personal computers or consoles; however, recent trends have seen the rise of cloud gaming services, which allow users to play games with essential devices and low-performance computers [15]. Several major players proposed their platforms (including, but not limited to, Google Stadia, Microsoft xCloud, Amazon Luna, and Nvidia GeForce Now), which are based on the same principle: at the core, the idea is to transmit the game's inputs to a dedicated cloud server rendering the game and sending back the resulting video and audio streams. This type of architecture works similarly to a streaming service, except that data is bidirectional, with inputs flowing from the player and the provider streaming AV data, which directly results from these inputs. As a result, the server is the only component that actively processes game data.

On the opposite side of the spectrum, in the same industry, we have in-browser games [30]. In these games, typically, client browsers receive the game data from the server and the client machine executes the received game logic and related audio-video rendering. Although this option looks similar to the classic setup, as the client machine is responsible for the heavy-duty computation in both cases, the case of in-browser games adds an important technological constraint: the game code must be *portable*, as the browser can access a set of technologies much stricter than those available on a general-purpose operating system. In fact, most of the games available as native executables for consoles or PC are not available for browsers: the problem here is more related to the technology stack than to the device capabilities.

Framing the problem definition of Sect. 2 into the videogame industry, we would like our game to be able to be played on a portable console, then be moved to a cloud or edge server when the battery gets low, and finally move into a desktop PC web browser—everything without the need for a restart of the application. Although such flexibility could be overkill for a gaming application (which would also have to find strategies to mitigate the impact of the latency introduced by the load shifting to the user, for instance by presenting a load screen), we believe it is not for the monitoring and correction of the behaviour of a large-scale distributed system—where similar issues apply.

3   Proposed Architecture

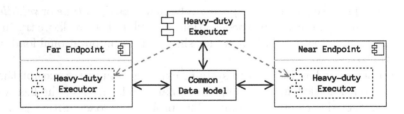

Fig. 1. Abstract architecture of the proposed system. Dashed lines indicate that the actual component (drawn with solid lines) can be in any of the potential states. In short, the proposal is to isolate the data model in order to have a common shared language, and have a mobile component that can be moved across devices (either because it is pre-installed and enabled on demand, or implemented with actual mobile code) capable of performing the heavy-duty computation.

The proposed architecture, summarised in Fig. 1 would be composed of four modules:

– **Far Endpoint** ($\mathcal{F}$)—*software* component, usually non-local, that provides means to perform the primary operations required on the target system through a well-defined API;

- **Near Endpoint** ($\mathcal{N}$)—*software* component the user interacts directly with, hence, running on a device the user has direct access to, whose goal is to interact with the Far Endpoint;
- **Common Data Model** ($\mathcal{M}$)—a formal (and serialisable) description of the data exchanged among all the components of the system;
- **Heavy-duty Executor** ($\mathcal{H}$)—software module responsible for performing resource-intensive computational tasks; this is the component that can be executed on either a Far or Near Endpoint instance, and, crucially, it can be moved from and to these endpoints at runtime, according to the model and assumptions presented in Sect. 2.

At the core of the idea is the isolation of the $\mathcal{H}$ component from the rest of the system and the definition of a common data model $\mathcal{M}$ that allows the $\mathcal{H}$ component to hop from one endpoint to another. Communication that would have happened in the form $\mathcal{N} \rightleftharpoons \mathcal{F}$ is actually translated into $\mathcal{N} \overset{M}{\rightleftharpoons} \mathcal{H} \overset{M}{\rightleftharpoons} \mathcal{F}$. Notice that $\mathcal{F}$ and $\mathcal{N}$ can, in principle, be as many as needed, as far as they can communicate and a single $\mathcal{H}$ is operational at a time for each $\mathcal{N}$ instance. Multiple $\mathcal{F}$ instances require more care, as $\mathcal{H}$ would need to be moved $\mathcal{F}$-to-$\mathcal{F}$ (possibly mediated by $\mathcal{N}$ instances): although possible in principle, we do not explicitly cover the case of multiple $\mathcal{F}$ in the architecture.

The architecture does not mandate the protocol used to move the $\mathcal{H}$ component between the $\mathcal{F}$ and $\mathcal{N}$ endpoints, but two abstract strategies are possible: (i) **copy and enable**: both the $\mathcal{F}$ and $\mathcal{N}$ endpoints have a copy of the $\mathcal{H}$ component, and only one of the two is active at a time; and (ii) **mobile code**: the $\mathcal{H}$ component is mobile code that is actually moved along the network. In the copy/enable strategy, the $\mathcal{H}$ component should be entirely separable from its state, constituting (part of) $\mathcal{M}$. Indeed, on a load shift, only the state is sent from the component hosting it previously to the new one. This strategy is the most straightforward to implement and the one that should have the better performance in terms of reactivity, but it requires careful design of $\mathcal{H}$ component, burdens both $\mathcal{F}$ and $\mathcal{N}$ with the duty to host a quiet copy of the software, and does not allow for runtime updates of $\mathcal{H}$. On the other hand, the mobile code strategy is more flexible, allows in principle for the runtime injection of updated versions of $\mathcal{H}$ (although this operation raises the question of how to ensure the integrity of the ongoing computation), but it is more complex to implement and is expected to impose more stress on the networking infrastructure when load-shifting.

3.1   Load-Shifting Spectrum: An Example

In this section, we briefly discuss how the proposed architecture may support the scenario described at the end of Sect. 2.1. We assume three devices in our system: (i) a battery-powered handheld console; (ii) a remote server located on the cloud or the edge; and (iii) a desktop PC. For the scenario to work as we expect, we need two instances of $\mathcal{N}$ located on the devices the user has direct access to (the handheld console and the desktop PC), and an instance of $\mathcal{F}$

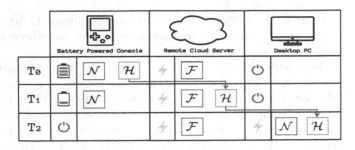

Fig. 2. Configuration and evolution of the example: the heavy-duty component $\mathcal{H}$, initially hosted on a handheld device, gets opportunistically shifted to the cloud, and then to a desktop PC-hosted web browser. Rows represent subsequent time steps, columns represent devices. Every column is split into two parts, on the left is the device status (off, battery level if turned on but off the power grid, on if on the power grid); on the right are the software components being executed.

located on the remote server. The situation and the evolution of the system are summarised in Fig. 2.

At the beginning of the scenario, the user is playing the game on the handheld console with a full battery, and the $\mathcal{H}$ component is located in the $\mathcal{N}$ component running on the handheld console. When the battery lowers, the load gets shifted to the remote server, and $\mathcal{H}$ is moved to the $\mathcal{F}$ component running remotely. Finally, if the user turns on the desktop PC and prefers to play the game there for higher responsiveness, they can start the local $\mathcal{N}$ component, then require a load-shift moving the $\mathcal{H}$ component locally.

3.2   Limitations and Technological Constraints

The first constraint we need to consider concerns $\mathcal{M}$: we notice that it must be serialisable and deserialisable in a way independent of the underlying runtime. Although cross-platform serialisation formats capable of representing most data structures across languages exist both in textual/human-readable form (e.g., JSON [17], YAML[1], etc.), and binary/efficiency-driven [25] form (e.g., Protocol Buffers [11], BSON[2], etc.) the requirement of being able to interoperate across possibly diverse runtimes imposes a clear and unambiguous specification. In turn, this implies that although the proposed architecture can be adopted for brand-new systems (in which the effort for a new design is due anyway), a significant effort would be required to retrofit many existing systems to the proposed architecture. Ultimately, for this architecture to be applicable, a pre-identification of all mobile parts is essential to maintain a consistent set of available resources and optimise the allocation of computational load. The need for such pre-identification stems from the fact that, in the general case, mobile parts

---

[1] http://yaml.org/spec/1.2/spec.pdf.
[2] https://bsonspec.org/spec.html.

may join or leave the system at any time, resulting in a constantly changing network topology. Consequently, a mechanism must be implemented to update the available resources in response to such changes.

However, the most significant constraint imposed by the proposed architecture is technological in nature and concerns the $\mathcal{H}$ component. By its very nature, $\mathcal{H}$ must be able to run as a module of $\mathcal{N}$ and $\mathcal{F}$ for which, however, we did not impose any constraint on the runtime or technology. This situation leads us to three potential cases.

Shared Technology/Runtime. By sheer luck or careful design, $\mathcal{N}$ and $\mathcal{F}$ share the same technology stack and runtime, and thus $\mathcal{H}$ can be realised once with a compatible technology and consumed by both $\mathcal{N}$ and $\mathcal{F}$. (note: they do not need to share the same programming language, as far as the executable form is portable across devices). This is the least interesting case, as in most cases modern runtimes provide means to move load between different network nodes. In these cases, the proposed architecture may not be needed (unless trying to anticipate changes).

Porting. For a more interesting case, we assume that $\mathcal{N}$ and $\mathcal{F}$ are based on entirely different and incompatible stacks and runtimes. For instance, $\mathcal{F}$ may be a Java/JVM or a native application running on a server, while $\mathcal{N}$ is a web application intended to run in-browser. One way to tackle this problem is to port $\mathcal{H}$ to both runtimes. This solution is adopted in some cases, with entire applications rewritten from their original runtime in JavaScript or TypeScript to target the browser[3]. Having multiple copies (one per runtime) of the same core application, however, is hardly ideal. Maintaining the code in sync is a tedious, expensive, and error-prone task, and while maintaining a porting may be worth it for a single application whose development is completed or slow-paced, the approach cannot scale to applications such as the primary target of this study: monitors for distributed systems, that are modern pieces of software running on the bleeding edge of technology and have a very fast-paced development.

Multi-target Technology. For the same case of the previous paragraph, a second option exists: selecting a technology for $\mathcal{H}$ capable of targeting both the runtimes of $\mathcal{N}$ and $\mathcal{F}$. This way, a single codebase exists for $\mathcal{H}$, with a multiple-target build process that produces two separate executables. Despite the simplicity of the approach on paper, it does present its fair share of challenges. The first one is, trivially, that the technology must be able to target both runtimes. This alone restricts the pool of suitable technologies, and the more the possible runtimes of $\mathcal{N}$ and $\mathcal{F}$, the more difficult it is to find a technology that can target all of them. A second relevant concern regards libraries and ancillary components, as they must be compatible with both runtimes. The second concern is often

---

[3] One notable example is the porting of the ioquake3 engine (https://ioquake3.org/) in JavaScript (http://www.quakejs.com/) as a proof-of-concept of the feasibility of running complex applications in the browser.

overlooked, but it is a significant one: if two different libraries are required for the same task to be achieved on two different runtimes, the host language and tooling must provide means to abstract over the differences and to select the specific implementation at runtime.

4   Proof of Concept

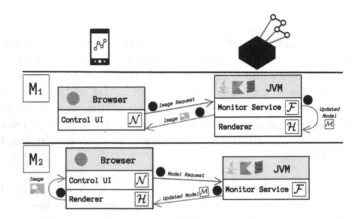

Fig. 3. Idea of the proof of concept. The $\mathcal{H}$ component can be moved at runtime to be hosted on the same host and platform of the $\mathcal{F}$ (in M_1) or to the same host and platform of the $\mathcal{N}$ (in M_2).

To exercise the proposed architecture and demonstrate its feasibility, we show a proof-of-concept implementation in the context of distributed monitoring. We want to build a monitor system for a distributed system that is composed of a set of nodes whose geographical distribution and logical relationships can change with time, thus whose rendering and control require significant computational effort. To stress the issues induced by incompatible runtimes, we choose a monitor service $\mathcal{F}$ implemented as a JVM-running application, and we want the monitoring and control access point $\mathcal{N}$ to be instead hosted in a web browser. Thus, our renderer component $\mathcal{H}$ must be able to run on both the browser and the JVM. In the former case, we want $\mathcal{N}$ to receive an instance of $\mathcal{M}$ and leverage $\mathcal{H}$ to render in-browser. In the latter case, instead, we want $\mathcal{N}$ to receive a pre-rendered image of the system built by $\mathcal{F}$ by running $\mathcal{H}$ on the JVM and displaying it in the browser. In this case $\mathcal{M}$ is already located on $\mathcal{F}$ and does not need to be moved. Figure 3 summarises the architecture of the proof-of-concept implementation.

4.1   Technology Selection

The presence of incompatible runtimes (the browser and the JVM) makes the trivial solution introduced in Sect. 3.2 infeasible. At the same time, given the problem at hand, we deemed the second solution (porting $\mathcal{H}$ to both runtimes) too expensive in terms of development resources and error-prone, as the same process would have needed to be written twice. Consequently, we were left with the third solution (multi-target technology).

An inspection of the mainstream technologies capable of targeting both the JVM and the browser with the same codebase restricted the pool of candidates to two languages and related frameworks: Scala [22] (with Scala.js [13,14]) and Kotlin-Multiplatform [16]. Both frameworks are currently maintained and have been used to develop interoperable tools that are found in the literature; two examples of interest to the community of distributed systems are, for instance, 2p-kt [10], a Prolog engine inspired by tuProlog [12] and written in Kotlin-multiplatform, and Scafi [8], a Scala implementation of the aggregate computing semantics [4] that also features a web-based playground [1]. An analysis of the two frameworks showed that they are similar from the point of view of the available features and documentation, and that the choice between them is mostly a matter of personal preference. In our proof-of-concept, we chose to use Kotlin-Multiplatform, mostly driven by the existence of a multiplatform library for serialisation developed and maintained by the Kotlin team (*kotlinx.serialization*[4]). We expected the serialisation to be critical in the development of the proof-of-concept, as the initial analysis highlighted the serialisation as a relevant issue in the implementation of the $\mathcal{M}$ component. In any case, we believe that the same proof-of-concept could be implemented in Scala as well, relying on third-party serialisation libraries.

Kotlin-Multiplatform. Kotlin features a mechanism for sharing pure Kotlin code across multiple platforms, enabling the development of platform-agnostic software modules, which are then compiled for a large variety of targets (including the JVM, Javascript, Android, and native binaries for several architectures and operating systems). The application or library code is split into multiple source sets, the root of which is the *common* one, consisting of core libraries and essential tools, enabling code to be platform-independent and functional on all systems. The other source sets contain platform-specific code variants targeting specific platforms. These variants (Kotlin/JVM, Kotlin/JS, and Kotlin/Native), offer platform-specific language extensions, libraries, and tools.

Of course, all dependencies (libraries) used in the common code must be available for all the target platforms. However, some functions may not be available for all targets, or may require a platform-specific implementation (for instance, a graphical component may require to be implemented using different toolkits). In these cases, Kotlin exposes a specific mechanism that allows declaring that some types or functions will be implemented in a platform-specific way: the `expect` keyword in the platform-agnostic code will mark the target as something not implemented yet, but that will be once a platform is selected. In the platform-specific code, the corresponding feature will be prefixed by the `actual` keyword (and the compiler will check that every platform-specific implementation provides all the `expect`ed types and functions).

---

[4] https://github.com/Kotlin/kotlinx.serialization.

4.2   System to be Controlled: $\mathcal{F}$

Building an entire cloud-edge continuum ecosystem was well beyond the scope
of this work, and we thus opted for controlling a system that could, in principle, abstract away the underlying system and expose the entities typical of the
problem we wanted to tackle: a simulator supporting the modelling of a situated
distributed system deployed on the cloud-edge continuum, and running within
an instance of the Java Virtual Machine (to comply with the requirements of
Sect. 4). Ideally, the target simulator must have a clean separation between the
renderer and the control components, so that the former can be easily replaced
with a different implementation. Additionally, to ease the development process,
we wanted the simulator to be open source and covered by a permissive license.

A natural choice was the Alchemist Simulator [24], which is well-known in the
DAIS community [23] and has been used in the past multiple times to simulate
systems akin to the ones we want to control. Alchemist comes with its own
Java-based rendering engine, but it also provides a clean separation between
the rendering and the control components, as witnessed by the existence of two
separate modules implementing two different graphical interfaces (one based on
Java Swing [21] and one based on JavaFX [26]).

In our proof-of-concept, the Alchemist simulator has been used as a Java
library, we created an additional module using Kotlin that translated the entities
exposed by the simulator in a multiplatform-friendly format. Such a component,
written in Kotlin-JVM, exposes the core simulator controls as a REST API to
allow for external control. The API also defines the protocol for load-shifting:
the $\mathcal{N}$ component is responsible to select whether it wants to run or offload $\mathcal{H}$,
and selects the appropriate route on $\mathcal{F}$.

4.3   Common Data Model: $\mathcal{M}$

The choice of the system to be controlled mandated the construction of the common data model. We selected a subset of the Alchemist model that we deemed
relevant for the purpose of the proof-of-concept, and implemented it in pure
Kotlin, in a format friendly to the serialisation library. In particular, we had
to create pure-Kotlin surrogate classes for the entities exposed by the simulator
that we needed to serialise, such as nodes and their position in the environment.
We notice that it is vital for the data model to be as minimal as possible: it represents the abstractions that are allowed to circulate between the components,
the more they are, the more complex the overall API and the more demanding
the overall system becomes.

4.4   Monitor/Controller: $\mathcal{N}$

Our monitor/controller, adhering to the requirements of Sect. 4, is a web-based
application with a simple UI displaying a rendering of the controlled the system.
The canvas is populated by the $\mathcal{H}$ component, which, depending on the position
of a switch, must migrate from the browser to the JVM-hosted $\mathcal{F}$ component.

Fig. 4. Sketch of the monitor/controller UI for the proof-of-concept.

To exemplify the work modes that we expect would be implemented on a real system, we design the interface to support three modes:

1. $\mathcal{H}$ **forcibly on** $\mathcal{N}$: $\mathcal{H}$ remains on $\mathcal{N}$, or migrates to $\mathcal{N}$ if it was on $\mathcal{F}$;
2. $\mathcal{H}$ **forcibly on** $\mathcal{F}$: $\mathcal{H}$ remains on $\mathcal{F}$, or migrates to $\mathcal{F}$ if it was on $\mathcal{N}$;
3. **Automatic**: depending on the system status, $\mathcal{H}$ migrates dynamically on $\mathcal{N}$ or $\mathcal{F}$. In the current proof-of-concept, the implementation is a very simple policy that migrates $\mathcal{H}$ depending on the available CPU cores. Real systems could adopt much more refined policies.

Provided the simplicity of the UI at hand, we decided to implement the monitor/controller from scratch based on the sketch depicted in Fig. 4.

In our proof-of-concept, the web application was developed using Kotlin/JS, and more specifically the React.js [29] framework port. The library provides a way to create reusable and self-contained components, encapsulating both the visual appearance and internal logic of a specific part of the application. To provide a responsive user experience, the application leverages components available as Javascript libraries on public repositories, such as React-Bootstrap [27]. As an implementation note, we add that we had to create custom adapter components to allow the typed use of the aforementioned libraries, since JavaScript is dynamically typed and Kotlin is statically typed.

4.5   Renderer: $\mathcal{H}$

In this section and in the remainder of the manuscript, we abuse the term "renderer" to refer to the component responsible for both rendering the system to be controlled and for interpreting and sending the command. The reason is that the most computationally-intensive operation is the rendering itself, and, in the spirit of load-shifting the most computationally-intensive operation, we tend to identify the heavy-load component with the most demanding operation it supports.

This component, which must be able to run both in the browser and the JVM, must be written in Kotlin multiplatform and use solely libraries available for both platforms. Although the ecosystem of multiplatform libraries is still in its infancy, we found a library suitable for rendering the system to be controlled (KorLibs/KorIM[5]). In this proof of concept, $\mathcal{H}$ is a renderer producing a graphical representation of a $\mathcal{M}$ representing the simulation environment.

4.6   Final Design

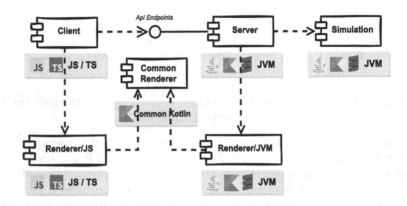

Fig. 5. UML component diagram of the implemented proof-of-concept.

The final incarnation of the proposed architecture is depicted in the UML Component Diagram of Fig. 5. The Server component represents $\mathcal{F}$ in the architecture, serving as a Web Server that provides API Endpoints. These endpoints are capable of executing commands on the Simulation components and retrieving data, which are then converted into structures compatible with the $\mathcal{M}$. The Client component represents $\mathcal{N}$, and is intended to communicate with the Server component via the previously mentioned API Endpoints. Both the $\mathcal{F}$ and $\mathcal{N}$ components rely on the platform-specific version of the Renderer component, which is the implementation of $\mathcal{H}$ in the architecture. Both $\mathcal{F}$ and $\mathcal{N}$ also need a platform-specific version of $\mathcal{M}$ to make the execution of $\mathcal{H}$ possible in every scenario. As mentioned, the implementation of $\mathcal{M}$ in pure Kotlin allows the serialization and deserialization operations to assure consistency when moving data between nodes. The state transfer protocol of the proof of concept is as follows: $\mathcal{F}$ always exposes *two* API endpoints, one for obtaining a representation of the model as an image, and the other to obtain the model as a serialised Kotlin object; when $\mathcal{N}$ decides to shift the load, it changes the API endpoint to which commands are sent. The proof-of-concept has been integrated within the main Alchemist repository[6], and is available within the official distribution.

---

[5] https://docs.korge.org/korim/.

[6] https://github.com/AlchemistSimulator/Alchemist.

5 Evaluation

In this section, we perform an evaluation of the proof-of-concept, discussing the viability of the proposed architecture to support interoperability and load-shifting. We initially perform a qualitative assessment, verifying that the proof-of-concept is able to render the system to be controlled and to shift the load between the browser and the JVM. We then perform a performance evaluation of the proof-of-concept, with the goal of comparing the operating conditions of the system when $\mathcal{H}$ is running on $\mathcal{N}$ and $\mathcal{F}$, and investigate how the system scales with larger and larger systems to monitor.

5.1 Test Environment and Qualitative Assessment

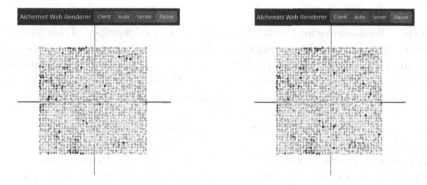

Fig. 6. Snapshots of the monitor/controller UI for the proof-of-concept, taken subsequently during the same experiment. Initially (left) the render (i.e., $\mathcal{H}$) is running within the client's browser (i.e., $\mathcal{N}$), then (right), at runtime, it is migrated to the server (i.e., $\mathcal{F}$), with no interruption, and no perceivable difference in the rendered image. In both snapshots, the warmer the color, the more the corresponding node had resource availability for itself.

We perform our evaluation by observing the behaviour of the proof-of-concept in a simulation of an existing reference system. We select an example from the Alchemist tutorial [23] in which a network of nodes coordinates for the use of a shared resource set. Resource usage tokens are generated and exchanged among neighbouring nodes ensuring that every resource is used by at most one node at a time. In the monitoring system, we investigate how many times every node had access to the resource, as the algorithm is not designed to guarantee fairness. For the sake of reproducibility, inspection, and to enable further research on the prototype, we provide an open-source repository with code, instructions, and support scripts for executing the experiment[7].

---

[7] https://github.com/AngeloFilaseta/DAIS-2023-alchemist-web-renderer.

Figure 6 depicts the current aspect of the monitor and the rendered monitored system, and shows that $\mathcal{H}$ can be moved dynamically back and forth from $\mathcal{N}$ to $\mathcal{F}$ without any interruption in the rendering process, thus complying with the requirements the architecture is designed to satisfy.

5.2   Performance Evaluation

Free Variables. We consider two free variables: (i) the number of nodes participating in the system, N ($N \in \mathbb{N}^+$), a proxy for the size of the monitored system; and (ii) the device hosting $\mathcal{H}$, either the same hosting $\mathcal{F}$ or hosting $\mathcal{N}$.

N has direct impact on the model size, and thus on the payload size when $\mathcal{H}$ is hosted on $\mathcal{N}$ (otherwise, the actual network payload is a rendered image, whose size is approximately constant). In our experiment, the serialized size of the model was at its minimum 46827 bytes ($N = 1600$) and 46827 bytes at its maximum ($N = 14400$).

Metrics. We measure four metrics to evaluate the performance of the system: (i) **rendering time**: the time required by $\mathcal{H}$ to complete its execution, this metric is meant to compare the raw performance of $\mathcal{H}$ across the available platforms and loads, we expect the execution on the JVM (i.e., $\mathcal{H}$ on $\mathcal{F}$) to be faster than on the browser (i.e., $\mathcal{H}$ on $\mathcal{N}$).); (ii) **serialisation time**: the time required by $\mathcal{F}$ to serialise $\mathcal{M}$ (if $\mathcal{H}$ is hosted on $\mathcal{N}$) or the rendered image (if $\mathcal{H}$ is being hosted on $\mathcal{F}$); this is a proxy metric for the load on the device hosting $\mathcal{F}$; (iii) **deserialisation time**: the time required by $\mathcal{N}$ to deserialise $\mathcal{M}$ (if $\mathcal{H}$ is hosted on $\mathcal{N}$) or the rendered image (if $\mathcal{H}$ is being hosted on $\mathcal{F}$), this is a proxy metric for the load on the device hosting $\mathcal{N}$; (iv) **total time**: the time required to complete an entire iteration, which includes all the previous metrics plus the network delay. We measure each metric five times, and we present the average result.

Results

We execute the experiment using two isolated containers on the same machine, an Intel® Core^{TM} i5-2520M CPU and 8GiB RAM. The results are presented and summarised in Fig. 7. As expected, allocating the load of $\mathcal{H}$ to $\mathcal{F}$ results in more consistent system performance with the growth of the monitored system. This is mainly driven by the higher efficiency of the JVM compared to the browser: besides being consistently faster in rendering the system (i.e., $\mathcal{H}$), it is also interestingly quicker in serialising the model as an image than it is in serialising it as plain JSON. We notice, however, that this last consideration is strictly dependent on the specific serialisation formats and libraries used, and may change with different implementations. We observe that hosting the $\mathcal{H}$ on the same node of $\mathcal{N}$ is pretty efficient for small systems, but it scales worse than hosting it on $\mathcal{F}$ with the monitored system size. This behaviour is evident both in the graph showing the deserialisation time and in the chart showing the overall system time.

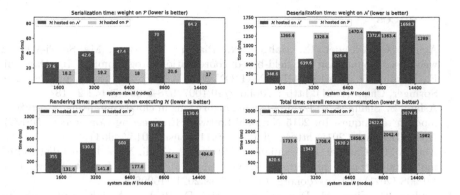

Fig. 7. Performance evaluation of the proof-of-concept. We measured proxy metrics for the load on $\mathcal{F}$ (top left), the load on $\mathcal{N}$ (top right), the cost of running $\mathcal{H}$ in either runtime (bottom left), and the overall cost of the system (bottom right).

6 Conclusion and Future Work

This paper introduces a novel architecture for developing monitoring and control systems for distributed systems deployed on a heterogeneous infrastructure in which the heavy-load part of the process can be moved across the devices. The architecture has been exercised by developing a proof-of-concept implementing the proposed architecture as an in-browser monitoring and control system for a simulator running on the JVM. The proof-of-concept shows that the proposed architecture is viable and can dynamically shift the load across different target runtimes, as far as the load that needs shifting can be executed on both platforms (or, suboptimally, get rewritten in multiple languages). The performance evaluation suggests that being able to shift the load dynamically across devices can be beneficial on heterogeneous systems.

Of course, although the proof-of-concept has been integrated with the Alchemist simulator, it is still very early in its development, which we plan to continue in the future. Additionally, we plan to study how the architecture can be adapted in case of multiple load sources, possibly impacting different metrics and thus requiring a dynamic assessment of the best location for the specific job. Finally, we believe that a lot of interesting research can be done in the area of automation of the load-shifting process: the current architecture and the prototype are designed to be used by a human operator, and show a single very simple strategy for the automated load-shift. However, much more complex mechanisms can be devised, possibly learning-enabled; we notice, in fact, that having multiple load sources scattered across a networked system at runtime may lead to pretty complex scenarios which could benefit from sophisticated automated approach.

Acknowledgements. The authors thank Gianluca Aguzzi for the fruitful discussions on languages, frameworks, and tools for multi-platform programming.

References

1. Aguzzi, G., Casadei, R., Maltoni, N., Pianini, D., Viroli, M.: ScaFi-Web: a web-based application for field-based coordination programming. In: Damiani, F., Dardha, O. (eds.) COORDINATION 2021. LNCS, vol. 12717, pp. 285–299. Springer, Cham (2021). https://doi.org/10.1007/978-3-030-78142-2_18
2. Aslam, S., Shah, M.A.: Load balancing algorithms in cloud computing: a survey of modern techniques. In: 2015 National Software Engineering Conference (NSEC). IEEE, December 2015. https://doi.org/10.1109/nsec.2015.7396341
3. Audrito, G., Casadei, R., Damiani, F., Stolz, V., Viroli, M.: Adaptive distributed monitors of spatial properties for cyber-physical systems. J. Syst. Softw. **175**, 110908 (2021). https://doi.org/10.1016/j.jss.2021.110908
4. Audrito, G., Viroli, M., Damiani, F., Pianini, D., Beal, J.: A higher-order calculus of computational fields. ACM Trans. Comput. Logic. **20**(1), 1–55 (2019). https://doi.org/10.1145/3285956
5. Bak, S., Menon, H., White, S., Diener, M., Kalé, L.V.: Multi-level load balancing with an integrated runtime approach. In: 18th IEEE/ACM International Symposium on Cluster, Cloud and Grid Computing, CCGRID 2018, Washington, DC, USA, May 1–4, 2018, pp. 31–40. IEEE Computer Society (2018). https://doi.org/10.1109/CCGRID.2018.00018
6. Bellavista, P., Corradi, A., Stefanelli, C.: Mobile agent middleware for mobile computing. Computer **34**(3), 73–81 (2001). https://doi.org/10.1109/2.910896
7. Bennaceur, A., et al.: Modelling and analysing resilient cyber-physical systems. In: SEAMS@ICSE 2019, pp. 70–76. ACM (2019). https://doi.org/10.1109/SEAMS.2019.00018
8. Casadei, R., Viroli, M., Aguzzi, G., Pianini, D.: ScaFi: a Scala DSL and toolkit for aggregate programming. SoftwareX **20**, 101248 (2022). https://doi.org/10.1016/j.softx.2022.101248
9. Chen, B., Cheng, H.H.: A runtime support environment for mobile agents. In: Volume 4a: ASME/IEEE Conference on Mechatronic and Embedded Systems and Applications. ASME (2005). https://doi.org/10.1115/detc2005-85389
10. Ciatto, G., Calegari, R., Omicini, A.: 2P-KT: a logic-based ecosystem for symbolic AI. SoftwareX **16**, 100817 (2021). https://doi.org/10.1016/j.softx.2021.100817
11. Currier, C.: Protocol buffers. In: Mobile Forensics – The File Format Handbook, pp. 223–260. Springer International Publishing, ham (2022). https://doi.org/10.1007/978-3-030-98467-0_9
12. Denti, E., Omicini, A., Ricci, A.: TUProlog: a light-weight prolog for internet applications and infrastructures. In: Ramakrishnan, I.V. (ed.) PADL 2001. LNCS, vol. 1990, pp. 184–198. Springer, Heidelberg (2001). https://doi.org/10.1007/3-540-45241-9_13
13. Doeraene, S.: Cross-platform language design in scala.js (keynote). In: Proceedings of the 9th ACM SIGPLAN International Symposium on Scala. p. 1. Association for Computing Machinery (2018). https://doi.org/10.1145/3241653.3266230
14. Doeraene, S., Schlatter, T., Stucki, N.: Semantics-driven interoperability between scala.js and JavaScript. In: Proceedings of the 2016 7th ACM SIGPLAN Symposium on Scala, pp. 85–94. Association for Computing Machinery (2016). https://doi.org/10.1145/2998392.2998404
15. Domenico, A.D., Perna, G., Trevisan, M., Vassio, L., Giordano, D.: A network analysis on cloud gaming: Stadia. GeForce now PSNow. Netw. **1**(3), 247–260 (2021). https://doi.org/10.3390/network1030015

16. Hagos, T.: Introduction to kotlin. In: Beginning Kotlin, pp. 1–20. Apress, November 2022. https://doi.org/10.1007/978-1-4842-8698-2_1
17. Ihrig, C.J.: JavaScript object notation. In: Pro Node.js for Developers, pp. 263–270. Apress (2013). https://doi.org/10.1007/978-1-4302-5861-2_17
18. Kanbar, A.B., Faraj, K.: Region aware dynamic task scheduling and resource virtualization for load balancing in IoT-fog multi-cloud environment. Future Gener. Comput. Syst. **137**, 70–86 (2022). https://doi.org/10.1016/j.future.2022.06.005
19. Milojicic, D.S.: The edge-to-cloud continuum. Computer **53**(11), 16–25 (2020). https://doi.org/10.1109/MC.2020.3007297
20. Mishra, S.K., Sahoo, B., Parida, P.P.: Load balancing in cloud computing: a big picture. J. King Saud Univ. Comput. Inf. Sci. **32**(2), 149–158 (2020). https://doi.org/10.1016/j.jksuci.2018.01.003
21. Newmarch, J.: Testing java swing-based applications. In: TOOLS 1999: 31st International Conference on Technology of Object-Oriented Languages and Systems, 22–25 September 1999, Nanjing, China, pp. 156–165. IEEE Computer Society (1999). https://doi.org/10.1109/TOOLS.1999.796479
22. Odersky, M.: Essentials of scala. In: Langages et Modèles à Objets, LMO 2009, Nancy, France, 25–27 mars 2009. vol. L-3, p. 2. Cépaduès-Éditions (2009)
23. Pianini, D.: Simulation of large scale computational ecosystems with alchemist: a tutorial. In: Matos, M., Greve, F. (eds.) DAIS 2021. LNCS, vol. 12718, pp. 145–161. Springer, Cham (2021). https://doi.org/10.1007/978-3-030-78198-9_10
24. Pianini, D., Montagna, S., Viroli, M.: Chemical-oriented simulation of computational systems with ALCHEMIST. J. Simul. **7**(3), 202–215 (2013). https://doi.org/10.1057/jos.2012.27
25. Popic, S., Pezer, D., Mrazovac, B., Teslic, N.: Performance evaluation of using protocol buffers in the internet of things communication. In: 2016 International Conference on Smart Systems and Technologies (SST). IEEE, October 2016. https://doi.org/10.1109/sst.2016.7765670
26. Robillard, M.P., Kutschera, K.: Lessons learned while migrating from swing to JavaFX. IEEE Softw. **37**(3), 78–85 (2020). https://doi.org/10.1109/MS.2019.2919840
27. Subramanian, V.: React-bootstrap. In: Pro MERN Stack, pp. 315–376. Apress (2019). https://doi.org/10.1007/978-1-4842-4391-6_11
28. Taherizadeh, S., Jones, A., Taylor, I.J., Zhao, Z., Stankovski, V.: Monitoring self-adaptive applications within edge computing frameworks: a state-of-the-art review. J. Syst. Softw. **136**, 19–38 (2018). https://doi.org/10.1016/j.jss.2017.10.033
29. Thakkar, M.: Introducing react.js. In: Building React Apps with Server-Side Rendering, pp. 41–91. Apress (2020). https://doi.org/10.1007/978-1-4842-5869-9_2
30. Vanhatupa, J.M.: Browser games for online communities. Int. J. Wirel. Mob. Netw. **2**(3), 39–47 (2010). https://doi.org/10.5121/ijwmn.2010.2303

EdgeEmu - Emulator for Android Edge Devices

Lyla Naghipour Vijouyeh[1]([✉]) [iD], Rodrigo Bruno[2] [iD], and Paulo Ferreira[1] [iD]

[1] University of Oslo, Oslo, Norway
{lylan,paulofe}@ifi.uio.no
[2] INESC-ID/Técnico, ULisboa, Portugal
rodrigo.bruno@tecnico.ulisboa.pt

Abstract. The number of mobile devices is rapidly outgrowing the current world population, making them the most popular medium to communicate and share information. In addition, applications that enable communication and data sharing still heavily rely on centralized networks. We believe that this problem is mainly due to the lack of tools to help programmers develop and test applications with many devices in edge environments.

To help programmers develop and test such distributed applications, we propose EdgeEmu, an Android distributed emulation testbed for mobile applications. EdgeEmu supports a high number of Android emulators participating in a large network by allowing them to remotely participate in the emulation, thus removing the scalability bottleneck that current Android testing infrastructure has. EdgeEmu is, therefore, not limited to locally deployed emulators as opposed to the standard Android SDK.

To study the performance of EdgeEmu, extensive evaluation through different scenarios has been conducted. Results demonstrate that EdgeEmu outperforms the standard Android SDK by approximately 59.1% in terms of emulation startup time when ten Android emulators are used. Evaluations also show promising results for low latency and negligible overhead when sending messages to and from different emulators.

Keywords: Android · Edge Networks · Wi-Fi Direct · Emulation · Peer-to-Peer · Bluetooth · Edge

1 Introduction

With more mobile devices than people in the world [1] and with their ever growing computational power, mobile devices have become the most pervasive computational platform for users [2] and are today an invaluable tool.

Supported by Department of Informatics, University of Oslo. Artifacts available in https://doi.org/10.5281/zenodo.7889579.

To achieve their full potential, mobile devices require communication with other mobile devices or external resources. As a consequence, almost every mobile application uses some form of communication technology. This is particularly true for data-sharing applications and location-based multiplayer games [3, 4]. These applications normally provide data sharing functionalities and users communications through the Internet, using Wi-Fi or broadband cellular network. For example, suppose two users want to share a file while being in the same physical location; to share this file, most data-sharing applications establish a connection to a remote central server or some kind of redirection service to exchange the data between the users, even though they are co-located. Using remote services instead of local ones increases latency, and globally increases the utilized network bandwidth. In addition, such applications have the limitation that they do not function properly in case of intermittent or limited Internet connection.

To avoid using an Internet connection when users are in proximity of each other, edge networks[1] provide an important shift regarding device-to-device communication and data sharing. Instead of relying on a central access point (router) with an Internet connection to establish communication and data transferring, mobile devices can use Peer-to-Peer (P2P) communication technologies like Bluetooth or Wi-Fi Direct [5] to achieve the same results when devices are near each other. Using such networks, applications can be developed to exploit user proximity.

When developing applications that take advantage of such edge networks, developing an application becomes an issue. One option is to gather dozens of Android devices in order to accurately develop it, while also having some device displacement to simulate users moving in and out of range with each other. This solution is not practical for several reasons such as cost, time, logistics, etc.

Android provides its own development tool kit with support for virtual emulation of Android devices called Android Studio [6]. However, this tool does not provide the necessary support to develop and test applications that apply the edge network paradigm. The Android Standard Development Kit (SDK) [7] does not implement multi-node emulation and displacement for the emulated Android devices, which is required to properly test edge network scenarios. Also, Android SDK supports up to 16 emulated Android devices, which limits the size of the emulated network. Other available network simulation and emulation tools (discussed in Sect. 2), offer no support for developing and testing such applications on top of the network created.

This lack of proper support for developing and testing edge-based applications forces developers to publish applications without proper testing or instead, drives developers away from using P2P communication technologies in favor of centralized communication technologies. To empower developers with the ability to test P2P communication-enabled applications with many Android devices, we propose EdgeEmu, a system capable of creating both small and large emulated edge networks, and support the development and testing of Android mobile

---

[1] In our paper, the term edge network represents a special case of **ad-hoc networks** that targets mobile devices that are co-located and involved in social interactions.

applications that follow such a paradigm. EdgeEmu transparently allows Android emulators to participate in large emulated networks while being hosted remotely, in different physical nodes (potentially in a public cloud).

Fundamental requirements to consider in the design of EdgeEmu include support several Android emulators (only limited by the number of machines) and negligible overhead in terms of latency and bandwidth. To support several emulators, EdgeEmu is designed and developed in a distributed manner. EdgeEmu has two main components. A Client that runs locally on the developer machine that is responsible for creating and modifying the network that is being emulated. A Server that runs on a machine that is used to run emulators that participate in the emulated network. The Server is responsible for managing the Android emulator instances that run on the same machine as the Server. A Client is able to connect to multiple Servers and use the emulators managed by them on the emulated network.

In order to examine the performance of EdgeEmu and show that it fulfills its design requirements, we performed a comprehensive evaluation. Results show that EdgeEmu can support up to 90 Android emulated devices when nine machines with 16 GB RAM are used for running EdgeEmu Servers. The number of supported emulators can vary depending on the number and specifications of the machines running EdgeEmu Servers. Also, results demonstrate that EdgeEmu components induce insignificant overhead in latency and bandwidth tests. In short, EdgeEmu is a new solution for the problem of developing and testing networks of Android emulated devices with negligible overhead in terms of latency and bandwidth while handling a large number of Android devices.

This paper is organized as follows. Section 2 provides a comprehensive study of the current network and cloud computing simulators and emulators, and testing frameworks. Section 3 presents some background information introducing the concept of Android Virtual Device (AVD), and Sect. 4 presents the architecture of EdgeEmu. A description of the implementation and an experimental evaluation are explained in Sect. 5 and Sect. 6, respectively. The paper concludes in Sect. 7.

2   Related Work

This section covers three areas we consider relevant to this work. First, network simulators/emulators (i.e., systems that help to develop and test network protocols). Then, we compare our work to simulators/emulators aimed at cloud/fog/edge environments; these are centered around simulating/emulating events between multiple devices (and not only network events). Finally, we also analyze other test frameworks, specially mobile application testing frameworks.

2.1   Network Simulators/Emulators

Network simulators are software solutions that can perform tasks in the abstract to demonstrate the behavior of a network and its components, without executing the real/concrete actions of these components or networks.

NS-2 [8] is an open-source, object-oriented TCL (OTcl [9]) script interpreter with a network simulation event scheduler. This network simulator can be used to extensively test new protocol solutions for various network paradigms. NS-2 is feature-rich when considering protocol and network testing, but it supports only a few number of network elements (nodes) that a network can have. The real problem that renders it incapable of supporting EdgeEmu is that NS-2 has no support for mobile application development and testing since it does not support mobile virtual devices.

NS-3 [10] was developed to improve the core architecture, software integration, models, and educational components of NS-2 while maintaining almost all features. The major improvement over NS-2 is using C++ programs or python scripts to define the simulations instead of relying on OTcl as its scripting environment. This made the tool significantly easier to use and build on top of. However, NS-3 still has the same problems as the ones identified on NS-2; it only supports a few nodes and shows no support for mobile application development and testing on top of the simulated network, thus making this tool unsuitable for EdgeEmu.

Other Network Simulation tools, e.g., GloMoSim [11], OMNET++ [12], J-Sim [13], or OPNET [14] provide distinct advantages and disadvantages [15,16]. Despite any desirable quality all these systems may have, they all fail to provide support for mobile application development and testing on top of the simulated network. This is crucial given the fundamental objective of this work in enabling the development of edge-based applications.

Network Emulators are normally available as hardware or software solutions that mimic the behavior of a network to functionally replace it. Network emulators allow network architects, engineers, and developers to attach end-systems such as computers to the emulated network; thus, such computers can act exactly as if they were attached to a real network [17]. This allows a user to accurately gauge an application's responsiveness, throughput, and quality of experience prior to applying or making changes or additions to a system. Most network emulation tools do not provide the necessary network characteristics to emulate edge-networks by allowing the network nodes to move within the network. In fact, all the network emulation tools that we analyzed show no support for mobile devices. Nevertheless, some of the tools present interesting solutions to system scalability; below we present the most relevant one.

NetWire [18] is a distributed network emulation system at the physical and MAC layer of the ISO/OSI network model. It follows a client/server architecture to the emulated network and the applications running on top. Each client (system or application) can interact with one or more servers emulating one or more networks. Network and node emulation can be spread among multiple workstations to distribute the omputational load, by connecting several network servers, drastically improving the system's scalability. However, NetWire has no support for virtual mobile devices or mobile applications being unable to emulate edge-networks since nodes within the network are stationary.

2.2   Fog, Edge and Cloud Simulators

In recent years, a number of simulators have been developed for paradigms such as cloud, edge, and fog computing in the context of, for example, Internet-of-Things (IoT) [19]. EmuEdge [20] is a hybrid emulator and extends Mininet alike systems to emulate edge computing platforms with heterogeneous nodes. CloudSim [21] is a popular simulator for cloud environments, allowing users to simulate cloud-related events such as resource provisioning. EdgeCloudSim [22] improves on CloudSim to target the specific demands of Edge Computing research. In particular, it provides support for the computation and networking abilities inherent to edge computing. CrowdSenSim [23] was developed to simulate Mobile Crowdsensing as it is an appealing paradigm [24].

Compared to current fog, edge, and cloud simulators, EdgeEmu presents a number of advantages when developing Android mobile applications. First, none of the above provide out-of-the-box support for testing Android devices with P2P protocols such as Wi-Fi Direct. Second, these solutions offer support only for simulation and not emulation and, as mentioned for network simulators, simulators provide less support for the design and development of applications. Finally, EdgeEmu provides a GUI that allows users to indicate where a smartphone is located and its path while moving.

2.3   Test Frameworks

There exist several commercial and open-source solutions to provide automated testing and enable the development of mobile applications (for example, MonkeyRunner [25], Appium [26], Expresso [27] and Robotium [28]). All of these tools present distinct advantages and disadvantages between them [29]. However, all these tools show the same problem, i.e., none is capable of emulating or simulating a network, which in turn renders them unable to properly execute tests for the particular case of applications that use edge-networks.

Termite [30,31] is an emulation test-bed that provides support for the development and testing of mobile applications. We found Termite to be the only system that has the ability to properly help to develop and test mobile applications running on emulated mobile devices on top of an emulated edge-network, with proper support for node displacement and interactions. Thus, Termite is the system that most closely resembles the one described in this work. However, it presents several downsides when it comes to developing and testing large edge-networks. To overcome the Android SDK limit that emulators can only communicate with up to 15 other emulators spawned in the same physical node, Bruno et al. propose using Android x86 [32]. Using Android x86, emulators can be distributed throughout different physical nodes and communicate with each other. However, using Android x86 images leads to several problems. First, using such images disrupts the normal Android development cycle as applications cannot be easily deployed and debugged with the help of Android Studio. Second, not all emulators (nor supported emulated features) that are available in the Android SDK are available in Android x86. Third, Termite requires a full deployment of a cloud infrastructure platform such as CloudStack [33] or OpenStack [34] to automatically deploy large edge-networks.

3   Android Virtual Devices and Networking

An Android Virtual Device (AVD) [35] defines the characteristics of an Android phone, tablet, Wear OS, Android TV, or Automotive OS device that is virtualized through an Android Emulator. In this particular work, an AVD configuration represents any Android mobile device. AVDs contain the hardware profile, system image, storage area, skin, and other properties that represent the Android device that developers may want to emulate. With this information, developers are able to create multiple unique Android emulators with the features described in their configuration.

When using the Android SDK, Android emulators run inside an isolated network inside the developer's machine. Each emulator instance runs behind a virtual router/firewall service that isolates it from the development machine, network interfaces, and from the Internet. According to the official Android Emulator networking documentation [36], there is a virtual router for each AVD instance that manages the 10.0.2.0/24 network address space; therefore, all addresses managed by the router are in the form of 10.0.2.N, where N is a number between 0 and 255. Addresses within such address space are pre-allocated by the emulator/router [36]. In this paper, Android emulators are also referred to as emulators hereafter.

So, consider a scenario in which we have an application running inside an AVD emulator instance (e.g., a smartphone app) communicating with some local service, listening on port 90 on IP 127.0.0.1 (in the developer's local machine). Note that both the developer machine's local network is 127.0.0.1 as well as the local network of the emulator; this is due to the fact that emulators have their own network environment. Thus, an application running in the smartphone cannot use the address 127.0.0.1:90 to access a local service on the developer machine; in fact, this would correspond to the emulators' loopback interface (a.k.a. 127.0.0.1). Instead, the application must use the special address 10.0.2.2 (10.0.2.2:90 to access the local service).

The developer machine sees each AVD emulator instance as a process that can be accessed via a pair of control ports. This pair of control ports (on the developer machine) correspond to: i) a default control port, and ii) an **Android Debug Bridge (adb)** client port. The default control port ranges from 5554 to 5584 (even numbers), and the **adb** client port ranges from 5555 to 5585 (odd numbers). Thus, each AVD emulator instance has a control port and an **adb** client port pair. These ports are sequentially attributed to each AVD emulator instance until the maximum port number is reached (5584 and 5585). Due to this limited port range, we can only have a maximum number of 16 emulators running simultaneously on the same developer machine.

It is important to note that the ports mentioned above only grant access to the AVD emulator instance and not to the mobile application that might be running inside; such ports are meant only to detect and configure the AVD emulator

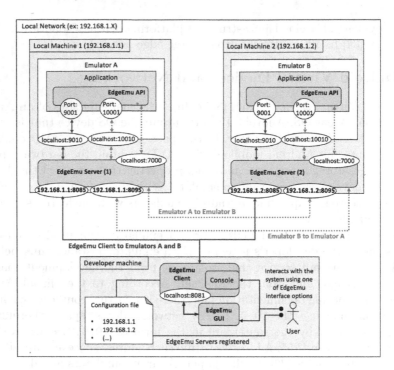

Fig. 1. EdgeEmu components and their interactions.

instance. The communication between any process on a developer machine network environment and an application running inside an AVD emulator instance requires that we first set a port redirection rule on the emulator.

To better understand how such redirection can be done, imagine that we wish to connect a client application process, running on the developer machine, to an application, acting as a server, inside emulator A that is listening on port 9001. As previously described, we know that processes (in this case the client application) outside the emulators network environment cannot reach or locally access the server application running inside it. To this end, we first need to set a port redirection rule on the emulator. This is done by using the **adb** command line tool (that communicates with the emulator through the **adb** client port) to perform a port redirection command: **redir add tcp:X:Y**. The port redirection command instructs the emulator A that any connections received on the port X in the localhost network of the developer machine must be redirected to the port Y inside the localhost network of the emulator A (X can be any available port number on the localhost network of the developer machine and Y is a port number of the application listening inside the emulator's network environment). Assuming X is 9010 and Y is 9001, the client application process accesses the server application inside the emulator A using the developer machine address **127.0.0.1:9010** which is redirected to the server port 9001 inside the emulator's localhost network.

4   EdgeEmu Emulation

We designed EdgeEmu to allow developers to develop and test applications that require large edge-networks. To that end, EdgeEmu is able to use emulators that are running across multiple machines (see Fig. 1).

As mentioned before, EdgeEmu consists of two main components: a Client and a Server. The **EdgeEmu Client** runs from a console window on the developer machine where the emulated network is created and modelled. User interactions with EdgeEmu can also be performed through this Client. The user is able to choose between two interface options: the text-based console where system interactions are done using written commands, or a GUI where system interactions are performed via interactive menus and options (see Sect. 5 for details).

An **EdgeEmu Server** needs to be running on each machine where we want to run emulators. In order for an EdgeEmu Client to access an EdgeEmu Server (and the emulators managed by it), the user must register them. This consists on writing the local IP addresses of the machines where EdgeEmu Servers are running on a configuration file provided to the EdgeEmu Client (see Fig. 1). This configuration file is a simple plain text file. Each local IP address of the EdgeEmu Servers' machines should be written in a separate line of the file. For instance, in Fig. 1, the local IP address of machine 1 is `192.168.1.1`. This IP address is automatically discovered by the EdgeEmu Server and can be used for accessing to EdgeEmu Server. Clearly, the user can assign arbitrary IP addresses to the EdgeEmu Servers via EdgeEmu Server-side plain text configuration file.

Thanks to the EdgeEmu Server, EdgeEmu is able to support a large number of emulators distributed across multiple machines. In EdgeEmu, emulators are identified using the machine's local IP address where they are running and two pairs of network addresses and port numbers. For example, in Fig. 1, emulator A is identified by the addresses `localhost:9010`, `localhost:10010`, and the local machine 1 network address (`192.168.1.1`); emulator B is identified by the addresses `localhost:9010`, `localhost:10010`, and the local machine 2 network address (`192.168.1.2`). These addresses are set by the EdgeEmu Servers. These addresses enable two types of interactions between EdgeEmu components: *Control Messages* and *Data Messages*.

Messages are sent from the EdgeEmu Client to the emulators following instructions given by the developer. These messages are called *Control Messages* (blue/solid arrows between the Client and the EdgeEmu servers 1 and 2) and are sent in two cases: i) when nodes (within the emulated network) move close to others, or ii) when P2P groups are formed between nodes (also within the emulated network). *Control Messages* contain information that allows the triggering of P2P events inside an application (e.g., using the Wi-Fi Direct API provided by Android). One such event is the creation of a P2P group with other target emulators. When such an event occurs, an application creates a socket connection with other group members, allowing them to communicate through *Data Messages* (green/dotted arrows). For example, taking into account Fig. 1, emulator A connects with the target emulator B. This connection is then

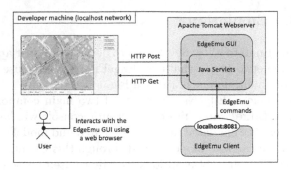

Fig. 2. EdgeEmu GUI implementation.

redirected to the application (running in emulator B) and received by a socket also opened by the EdgeEmu API on port 10001.

As illustrated in Fig. 1, the EdgeEmu Client connects with each registered EdgeEmu Server through the addresses `192.168.1.1:8085` and `192.168.1.2:8085`. Note that the port value 8085 is predefined on the EdgeEmu Server but can be changed to any other port value chosen by the user through the EdgeEmu Server-side plain text configuration file. With these connections, the EdgeEmu Client is then able to discover and use the emulators that are running on each EdgeEmu Server machine. These connections are used by the EdgeEmu Client to send the *Control Messages* to emulators using the EdgeEmu Servers as intermediaries.

As already mentioned, emulators can communicate with each other by using EdgeEmu to create a socket connection with the group member (the socket connection is created using the addresses of each emulator, provided within the control message information). This connection is performed with the EdgeEmu Server(s) of each emulator as intermediaries. In Fig. 1 we can see this and the addresses used by looking at the green/dotted arrows.

Lastly, it is worth mentioning that EdgeEmu easily allows the user to manage the emulators' life cycle (create, destroy, start, stop and install, and start applications) from the EdgeEmu Client. This is crucial for EdgeEmu to support several Android emulators as it allows a user to create and manage a large number of them (and the applications running inside) distributed across multiple machines from a single control point.

5   Implementation

Most components in EdgeEmu were implemented using Java version 17. We use this language to guarantee that it can easily run on any platform and that it is easily extendable. In addition, as Android libraries and applications are largely written in Java [37], it was a natural choice.

The EdgeEmu GUI runs on top of an Apache Tomcat Server version 9 and the interface logic is implemented using JavaScript ES6. We opted for JavaScript as it allows the interface logic to run across any modern web browser (Google Chrome, Firefox, Safari, etc.). EdgeEmu supports both Google Maps API [38] and OpenStreetMap API [39] and gives users an option to select their preference. We chose Google Maps due to its extensive documentation and features and OpenStreetMap as it is free.

The GUI performs two types of communications with the EdgeEmu Client: i) requesting data (e.g., requesting emulators to be used on the emulated network), and ii) sending data (e.g., sending Control Messages to the target emulators or commands to start new emulators). These communications (illustrated in Fig. 2) are implemented using HTTP GET and POST requests and the data is formatted using JSON objects. These requests are sent from the web browser to a web service (implemented using Java Servlets running inside the Tomcat Server) that translates them to EdgeEmu commands (similar to those when a user uses the console interface). The commands are then sent from the Servlets to the EdgeEmu Client (through a socket connection on `localhost:8081`) to be processed.

6 Evaluation

In this section, we compare EdgeEmu with Termite, a previous existing open-source system (described in Sect. 2). Looking both at Termite and EdgeEmu's architectures, we can identify that the main difference is the EdgeEmu Server and EdgeEmu Client components (both used to relay messages). These components, both in EdgeEmu, completely change how messages are exchanged within the system: both when we consider the communication protocols between the EdgeEmu Client and the emulators, and also between emulators. In fact, in Termite, messages are exchanged directly from the sender emulator to the receiver. In EdgeEmu, such communication is not direct because the EdgeEmu Server acts as a middle point responsible for redirecting messages sent from the EdgeEmu Client to the target emulators and messages exchanged between emulators.

To compare both systems and focus on the most differentiating aspects, we developed two tests: i) the Ping Test, a latency test (see Sect. 6.2) that measures the time it takes to send a ping message from the EdgeEmu Client to the emulators and receive a response; ii) the File Sharing Test (see Sect. 6.3), a bandwidth test that measures the time it takes to send a large message from one emulator to another and receive a response.

We also conduct additional experiments using latency and bandwidth tests where an increasing number of emulators is either deployed locally or remotely (see Sect. 6.4). First, we run both tests on Termite and EdgeEmu while running locally (i.e., all system components and emulators run on the same developer machine). Then, we execute the same tests on EdgeEmu, this time running all the necessary AVD emulator instances remotely. This means that on one machine we run the EdgeEmu Client while the necessary emulators run on multiple remote machines. On each remote machine, there is an instance of the EdgeEmu Server.

The number of emulators running on each machine varies according to the test being performed.

6.1 Testing Environment

When performing the tests locally, all elements of both Termite and EdgeEmu execute on a single cluster node. All cluster nodes run Ubuntu 18.04, and are equipped with an Intel Core i5-4460 3.20 GHz (Quad-core) CPU, with 16 GB RAM. All the used emulators correspond to a Pixel2 Android phone running Android 5.1 with API 21. This Android version and API allow us to cover more than 99% of the existing smartphones [40]. When performing tests where the AVD emulators' instances are distributed throughout different cluster nodes, the EdgeEmu Client executed in a local MacBook Pro with macOS Catalina 10.15.7, featuring a (Dual-Core) Intel Core i5 2,7 GHz CPU (4 threads), with 8 GB of RAM.

We never run more than ten emulator instances simultaneously on a single cluster node. This was done due to memory constraints as Android emulators have high memory requirements, and over committing memory rapidly slows down emulators' response times. In fact, running 10 emulators consumes approximately 13GB of RAM and utilizes 40% of CPU. Thus, with a cluster node, having 16GB of RAM (14GB usable), running more than ten emulators starts to severely impact system speed and responsiveness.

6.2 Ping Test

The Ping test was developed to evaluate EdgeEmu Server's latency impact when messages are exchanged between an EdgeEmu Client and the emulators. The

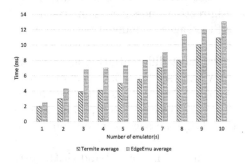
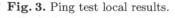

Fig. 3. Ping test local results.

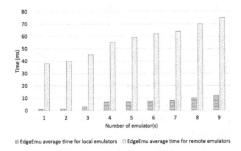

Fig. 4. Ping test remote results.

test consists of measuring the time it takes to send a single message from the EdgeEmu Client component to an increasing number of AVD emulator instances. Thus, we created a test script that would send a message to each emulator and measured the time that each message took to be received and a response being sent. Starting with one emulator instance, we executed the test script until the variance of time values obtained becomes less than 10%. In order to ensure the validity of results, we performed the test script at least ten times. We then increased the number of emulators and performed the same test until a maximum of ten emulators instances was reached. After all tests were concluded, we calculated the average value of each test.

As explained before, the test was performed in two different scenarios. First, we executed the tests running all system components and the emulators locally (i.e., in a single machine). Then, we performed the same test but instead of increasing the number of emulators that run locally, we increased the number of remote machines being used with each machine running a single emulator.

The results obtained when performing the Ping test locally on Termite and EdgeEmu can be seen in Fig. 3. Results show that EdgeEmu Server has a negligible impact on the time that it takes to send/receive the ping messages (less than 3 milliseconds). This allows us to conclude that EdgeEmu presents a performance similar to Termite on this type of communication within a local environment.

For the tests conducted with each emulator running in different remote cluster nodes, the results show (see Fig. 4) there is a performance impact when compared with the local EdgeEmu test results (around 40 to 70 milliseconds depending on the number of remote machines). The reason for this increase is that messages are exchanged over the Internet between EdgeEmu Client and the cluster nodes. This is expected and we believe that 40–70 ms of latency does not compromise the usability of the system as many real systems that operate over the Internet also include similar latencies.

6.3   File Sharing Test

We now evaluate EdgeEmu bandwidth impact when exchanging messages between two emulators. The test consists in measuring the bandwidth between

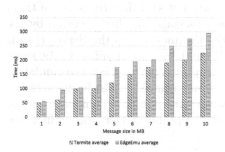

Fig. 5. File Sharing test local results.

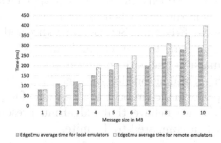

Fig. 6. File Sharing test remote results.

two emulators by measuring the time that takes to send a varying size file (1 MB to 10 MBs) from one emulator to another (when they are part of a P2P group). To that end, we create an Android mobile application (running in emulators) that detects the creation of the P2P group and automatically sends the file to the other group member (i.e., the other emulator). The application then measures the time between sending the file and receiving a response from the other group member. In order to trigger this P2P event between the two emulators, we run a script using EdgeEmu commands that emulate the creation of the P2P group between two emulators running the app previously mentioned. We ran this test script until the variance of time values obtained was less than 10%. To respect the reliability of the results, the test script was executed at least 10 times. Similar to the Ping Test, this test was performed in two different scenarios. After all tests are finished, we calculate the average time value for each test.

Results obtained for the File Sharing test on Termite and EdgeEmu with both emulators running on the same machine can be seen in Fig. 5. The results show that EdgeEmu Server has a negligible impact on the time that messages take to be sent from one emulator to another (an increase of around 30 milliseconds per MB). We conclude that EdgeEmu presents a similar performance as Termite on this type of communication when emulators are running on the same machine.

For the tests conducted on EdgeEmu with each AVD emulator instance running on different cluster machines, the results show (see Fig. 6) that there is a performance impact when compared with the local EdgeEmu test results: an increase of 20–109 milliseconds per MB when compared with the results obtained on EdgeEmu using local emulators. The reason for this time increase is the fact that the messages sent from one emulator to another are done from two different cluster machines over the network. Nevertheless, we consider this overhead to be completely normal as it is mostly due to network communication latency and not due to EdgeEmu. Furthermore, we expect real applications to send small to medium size files as sending large files through a P2P connection (Wi-Fi Direct) is not recommended due to the unstable nature of this type of communication (devices come in and out of proximity of each other depending on their speed).

In conclusion, EdgeEmu Server has a negligible impact on the time that an emulator takes to send and receive messages from and to another emulator. This happens due to the fact that messages are not sent directly between them (as is the case when using Termite). Instead, messages are first received by the local EdgeEmu Server and redirected to the destination (to the Server that is managing the target emulator). When both emulators are running on the same machine the performance impact is low; the impact is higher when the emulators are running on different machines. However, we believe that in both cases the performance impact is acceptable for the communication paradigm we are using and we believe that EdgeEmu presents an acceptable performance difference when compared to Termite.

6.4   Number of Emulators

The number of AVD emulator instances we can use within the emulated network running the application we wish to develop and test has an obvious impact on EdgeEmu performance. We have previously mentioned that when using Termite we need to use the Android Studio AVD Manager or user-made scripts to create and manage the emulator instances. We also know that due to Android SDK limitations we can only start a maximum of 16 emulators instances at the same time on a single machine. As such, when using Termite, we are only able to create an emulated network with a maximum of 16 target emulators. This number assumes that the local machine has all the resources needed for that purpose, which is not realistic for most commodity developer laptops and desktops.

On the contrary, with EdgeEmu, one can now create and manage all AVD emulator instances directly from an EdgeEmu Client. This removes the need to use Android AVD Manager or user-made scripts to manage the emulators. Using EdgeEmu also provides a solution to the Android SDK limitation on the maximum number of emulators we can run locally. This is done by allowing a user to create the emulated network on one machine and run the AVD emulator instances distributed across other machines. As a result, users can create much larger emulated networks.

Local Deployment: This test evaluates the time that it takes to launch an increasing number of AVD emulator instances running a test application using both Termite and EdgeEmu. The test consists of measuring the time it takes to launch a selected number of emulator instances, installing an application on each emulator and running it.

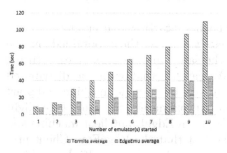 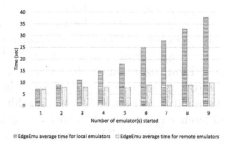

Fig. 7. Local Deployment results for Termite and EdgeEmu.

Fig. 8. Startup time for local and remote emulators using EdgeEmu.

To perform this test on Termite we created a simple script file using Termite commands to perform the same actions of launching the emulators, installing the applications, and running them. Starting with one emulator instance to a maximum of 10, the test runs until the variance between time values obtained was less than 10%. We ran the test script at least 10 times to ensure the validity of the results. This test was performed on a single cluster machine. Results for this test are shown in Fig. 7. By looking at the plot it is possible to see that EdgeEmu presents a significant improvement in the time that it takes to launch the emulators, install the applications and start them. The reason for this improvement is due to the fact that Termite starts the emulator instances sequentially while EdgeEmu starts all emulator instances in parallel. We can see

124 L. N. Vijouyeh et al.

this by considering that the time improvement when we use EdgeEmu is greater when the number of emulators used increases.

Distributed Deployment: From the previous test results we were able to show how EdgeEmu speeds up the deployment of the increasing number of emulators and applications on a single machine. However, because we are running all the emulator instances on a single machine, we are still limited by its performance and the hard limit imposed by Android SDK of 16 emulators instances running at the same time on the same machine.

To truly show how EdgeEmu behaves with an increasing number of emulators, we developed a similar application to the previous one but now each emulator instance runs on a different cluster machine. To perform the test, we used a similar script file as the one created for the Local Deployment test, but now we distribute the emulators across multiple cluster machines. This script file was loaded on EdgeEmu Client and the emulators started on remote machines.

First, we started by measuring the time it takes to deploy a single emulator per machine, installing the template application and starting it. Then, we perform the same test but this time we deployed 10 emulators instances per remote machine. With 9 cluster machines, we were able to launch a total of 90 emulators, a drastic improvement over the maximum of 16 emulators that one can run when using Termite.

In Fig. 8 we show the values obtained when starting one emulator across the 9 cluster machines, and compare these values to those obtained on the Local Deployment test, where we started the same amount of emulators (using EdgeEmu) on a single cluster machine. We can see that with the distributed approach, the time it takes to start one emulator on a single machine and start 9 emulators across 9 different machines is approximately the same (the slight difference is because of the network delay between EdgeEmuClient machine and cluster machines). This happens due to the fact that the EdgeEmu Client processes/sends the start commands to the EdgeEmu Servers on multiple machines at the same time. Thus, with EdgeEmu it is possible to explore the inherent parallelism of a distributed system.

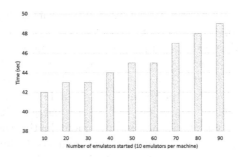

Fig. 9. The time that it takes to start 10 emulators across the 9 cluster machines.

This parallel processing is again shown on the results obtained when starting 10 emulators across each one of the 9 cluster machines (see Fig. 9). As expected, starting 10 emulators on a single machine takes approximately the same time as starting 90 emulators across 9 different machines (with 10 emulators per machine).

Finally, by looking at Fig. 9 and comparing the results obtained to those that we presented on the Local Deployment test, we can see that starting 90 emulators takes less time than to start 10 emulators on Termite (using Android Studio which starts the emulators sequentially). With these results, we can easily conclude that EdgeEmu offers better performance when compared to Termite.

7   Conclusion

On the one hand, network simulation and emulation tools available today do not provide sufficient support to develop and test edge-based applications. On the other hand, existing tools that emulate edge-based networks lack the necessary network layer where tests must be performed. Termite, the closest system to EdgeEmu, does not perform well with an increasing number of Android emulators.

This work presents EdgeEmu. It proposes a distributed system architecture where the emulated network and the emulated Android devices used can run on distinct machines. The user is able to create the emulated network on one machine and offload/distribute the computational load of running a large number of emulators throughout other machines. This allows the creation of much larger emulated networks where more complex applications can be developed and tested.

References

1. W3Techs: GSMA intelligence. Accessed Feb 2023. https://www.gsmaintelligence.com
2. STATISTICA: Mobile internet usage worldwide - statistics and facts. Accessed Feb 2023. https://www.statista.com/topics/779/mobile-internet
3. Baek, S., Ahn, J., Kim, D.: Future business model for mobile cloud gaming: the case of South Korea and implications. IEEE Communications Magazine, pp. 1–7 (2023)
4. Kaisar, S., Kamruzzaman, J., Karmakar, G., Rashid, M,M.: Decentralized content sharing in mobile ad-hoc networks: a survey, Digital Communications and Networks (2022)
5. Wi-Fi Alliance: Portable Wi-Fi that goes with you anywhere. Accessed Feb 2023. https://www.wi-fi.org/discover-wi-fi/wi-fi-direct
6. Google: Android studio the official integrated development environment (ide) for android app development. Accessed Feb 2023. https://developer.android.com/studio
7. Google: Android standard development kit. Accessed Feb 2023. https://developer.android.com/studio

8. NS-2: The network simulator - NS-2. Accessed Feb 2023. https://nsnam. sourceforge.net/wiki/index.php/Main_Page
9. Wetherall, D.: OTcl - MIT object Tcl. Accessed Feb 2023. https://otcl-tclcl. sourceforge.net/otcl/
10. NS-3: ND-3 network simulator. Accessed Feb 2023. https://www.nsnam.org
11. Bajaj, L., Takai, M., Ahuja, R., Tang, K., Bagrodia, R., Gerla, M.: Glomosim: A scalable network simulation environment. UCLA computer science department technical report (1999)
12. OMNeT++: OMNeT++ discrete event simulator. Accessed Feb 2023. https:// omnetpp.org
13. J-Sim: J-Sim network simulator. Accessed Feb 2023. https://www.kiv.zcu.cz/j-sim/
14. OPNET Optimum Network Performance: OPNET network simulator. Accessed Feb 2023. https://opnetprojects.com/opnet-network-simulator/
15. Chengetanai, G., O'Reilly, G.B.: Survey on simulation tools for wireless mobile ad hoc networks. In: IEEE International Conference on Electrical, Computer and Communication Technologies (2015)
16. Mallapur, S., Patil, S.: Survey on simulation tools for mobile ad-hoc networks. RACST - Int. J. Comput. Netw. Wirel. Commun. 2(2), 2250–3501 (2012)
17. Imran, M., Said, A.M., Hasbullah, H.: A survey of simulators, emulators and testbeds for wireless sensor networks. In: International Symposium on Information Technology (2010)
18. Enrico, C., Renzo, D.: The netwire emulator: a tool for teaching and understanding networks. SIGCSE Bull. 33(3), 153–156 (2001)
19. Markus, A., Kertesz, A.: A survey and taxonomy of simulation environments modelling fog computing. Simulation Modelling Practice and Theory, vol. 101, p. 102042, 2020, modeling and Simulation of Fog Computing. https://www.sciencedirect.com/science/article/pii/S1569190X1930173X
20. Zeng, Y., Chao, M., Stoleru, R.: EmuEdge: a hybrid emulator for reproducible and realistic edge computing experiments. In: 2019 IEEE International Conference on Fog Computing (ICFC), June 2019, pp. 153–164 (2019)
21. Calheiros, R.N., Ranjan, R., Beloglazov, A., De Rose, C.A.F., Buyya, R.: Cloudsim: A toolkit for modeling and simulation of cloud computing environments and evaluation of resource provisioning algorithms. Softw. Pract. Exper. 41(1), 23–50 (2011). https://doi.org/10.1002/spe.995
22. Sonmez, C., Ozgovde, A., Ersoy, C.: Edgecloudsim: An environment for performance evaluation of edge computing systems. In: Second International Conference on Fog and Mobile Edge Computing (FMEC), 2017, pp. 39–44 (2017)
23. Fiandrino, C., Capponi, A., Cacciatore, G., Kliazovich, D., Sorger, U., Bouvry, P., Kantarci, B., Granelli, F., Giordano, S.: Crowdsensim: a simulation platform for mobile crowdsensing in realistic urban environments. IEEE Access 5, 3490–3503 (2017)
24. Ganti, R.K., Ye, F., Lei, H.: Mobile crowdsensing: current state and future challenges. IEEE Commun. Mag. 49(11), 32–39 (2011)
25. Google: Monkeyrunner user guide. Accessed Feb 2023. https://developer.android. com/studio/test/monkeyrunner
26. JS Foundation: Appium automation for apps. Accessed Feb 2023. https://appium. io
27. Open Source: Expresso framwork. Accessed Feb 2023. https://developer.android. com/training/testing/espresso

28. RobotiumTech: Robotium user scenario testing for android. Accessed Feb 2023. https://github.com/RobotiumTech/robotium
29. Gunasekaran, S., Bargavi, V.: Survey on automation testing tools for mobile applications. Int. J. Adv. Eng. Res. Sci. **2**(11), 2349–6495 (2015)
30. Bruno, R., Santos, N., Ferreira, P.: Termite: emulation testbed for encounter networks. In: Mobiquitous 2015 Proceedings of the 12th EAI International Conference on Mobile and Ubiquitous System: Computing, pp. 31–40 (2015)
31. Santos, N., Ferreira, P., Bruno, R.: Termite: Emulation testbed for encounter networks. Accessed Feb 2023. https://nuno-santos.github.io/termite/index.html
32. Android-x86: Android-x86 - run android on your PC. Accessed Feb 2023. https://www.android-x86.org/
33. Apache CloudStack: Apache CloudStack - open source cloud computing. Accessed Feb 2023. https://cloudstack.apache.org/
34. Open Source Cloud Computing Infrastructure. Accessed Feb 2023. https://www.openstack.org/
35. Google: Create and manage virtual devices. Accessed Feb 2023. https://developer.android.com/studio/run/managing-avds
36. Google: Set up android emulator networking. Accessed Feb 2023. https://developer.android.com/studio/run/emulator-networking
37. Pam: Java Mobile Applications Development, November 2021. https://www.webiotic.com/java-mobile-applications-development-what-you-need-to-know/
38. Google: Google maps platform documentation. Accessed Feb 2023. https://developers.google.com/maps/documentation
39. Coast, S.: OpenStreetMap Wiki. Accessed Feb 2023. https://wiki.openstreetmap.org/wiki/Main_Page
40. Google: Android API levels. Accessed Feb 2023. https://apilevels.com/

Author Index

Printed in the United States
by Baker & Taylor Publisher Services